MW01002785

MARK

TWAIN

FOR

DOG

LOVERS

Mark Twain is widely credited with saying, "The more I learn about people, the more I like my dog." He liked dogs well enough, but there is no evidence he ever said anything like that himself. The remark actually may have originated in France, with either Voltaire or Madame de Stael, long before his time. The St. Bernard posing with Mark Twain in this 1904 picture belonged to his daughter Jean, his family's most ardent dog lover. Jean probably took the dog's name, "Prosper le Gai," from a character in Maurice Henry Hewlett's 1898 novel The Forest Lovers. MARK TWAIN HOUSE AND MUSEUM, HARTFORD, CONNECTICUT

MARK TWAIN FOR DOG LOVERS

True and Imaginary Adventures
WITH MAN'S BEST FRIEND

Edited by
R. KENT RASMUSSEN

GUILFORD, CONNECTICUT

An imprint of Rowman & Littlefield

Distributed by NATIONAL BOOK NETWORK

Copyright © 2016 R. Kent Rasmussen

Excerpt from Samuel L. Clemens to Jane Lampton Clemens, 24 July 1887.
Excerpt from Samuel L. Clemens to Joe Twichell, 25 April 1892.
Excerpt from Samuel L. Clemens to William Dean Howells, 12–13 May 1899.
Miscellaneous Writings: Previously Unpublished Letters, Manuscript Letters, and Literary Manuscripts Available in the Mark Twain Papers, by Mark Twain, © 2001 by the Mark Twain Foundation. Published by the University of California Press.

Excerpt from "'The Enchanted Sea Wilderness," *Mark Twain's "Which Was the Dream?" and Other Symbolic Writings of the Later Years*, by Mark Twain, edited by John S. Tuckey. © 1966 by the Mark Twain Foundation. Published by the University of California Press.

Excerpt from *Autobiography of Mark Twain: The Complete and Authoritative Edition, Volume 1*, by Mark Twain, edited by Harriet Elinor Smith, pp. 416–417. © 2011 by the Mark Twain Foundation. Published by the University of California Press.

Photographs and illustrations courtesy of: The Mark Twain Papers, The Bancroft Library, University of California, Berkeley; The Mark Twain House & Museum, Hartford, Connecticut; Library of Congress, Prints and Photographs; collection of Kevin Mac Donnell, Austin, Texas; and collection of the editor.

All rights reserved. No part of this book may be reproduced in any form or by any electronic or mechanical means, including information storage and retrieval systems, without written permission from the publisher, except by a reviewer who may quote passages in a review.

British Library Cataloguing in Publication Information Available

Library of Congress Cataloging-in-Publication Data Available

ISBN 978-1-4930-1958-8 (cloth)
ISBN 978-1-4930-2710-1 (e-book)

∞™ The paper used in this publication meets the minimum requirements of American National Standard for Information Sciences—Permanence of Paper for Printed Library Materials, ANSI/NISO Z39.48-1992.

To the memory of

JEAN CLEMENS (1880–1909),

who deeply loved both

dogs and Mark Twain

Jean Clemens in Vienna on July 25, 1898, the day before she turned eighteen, holding the pet Manchester terrier she called "the Professor." In early 1899, she inscribed a copy of this photo to a friend, "Much love from the Professor." Six months earlier, she had inscribed another photo taken at the same time, "With the Professor's warmest snarls." MARK TWAIN HOUSE AND MUSEUM, HARTFORD, CONNECTICUT

CONTENTS

INTRODUCTION

In 1935, syndicated columnist George Matthew Adams published a celebration of what he simply called "Good Things." Because the next day, November 30, was the 100th birthday of Samuel L. Clemens—the man better known as Mark Twain—the first good thing he praised was "the memory of a man who was one of the world's greatest benefactors—Mark Twain." How did Adams believe Mark Twain benefitted the world? By using "his great talents to lessen the troubles of mankind and to impress upon people that humor is the greatest medicine in the world." That made sense. In 1907, when the University of Oxford had conferred an honorary doctor of laws degree on Mark Twain, it thanked him for shaking the sides of the world with laughter—precisely what Mark Twain did and still does today.

The next "good thing" on Adams's list was dogs. He described how no one could stroll by a pet store without stopping to watch dogs cavorting in the window, adding "that the love of a dog is universal." Something similar might be said of the love for Mark Twain. Indeed, the same year Oxford honored him, the great American inventor Thomas Edison remarked, "An average American loves his family. If he has any love left over for some other person he generally selects Mark Twain."

Adams's pairing of Mark Twain with dogs was inspired. Both make people happy and both are almost universally loved. Moreover, as this book will amply show, Mark Twain and dogs have much closer connections than is generally realized. Mark Twain is famous for his love of cats, but he also had a strong affection for dogs. When his oldest daughter, Susy, was eleven, she said of her parents, "Mama loves morals and papa loves cats." That was unquestionably true, but Mark Twain also loved *all* animals and greatly admired dogs. "The dog is a gentleman," he wrote in an 1899 letter to his friend William Dean Howells. "I hope to go to his heaven, not man's." That's a sentiment he never expressed about cats.

What Mark Twain most liked about cats was their fierce independence—their self-reliance and refusal to be enslaved. In a private notebook he wrote, "Of all God's creatures there is only one that cannot be made the slave of the lash. That one is the cat." The same certainly cannot be said of dogs. However, as many of the stories in this book will show, Mark Twain admired dogs for their friendly dispositions and strong loyalty to their masters. "We cannot all be as good & sweet & lovely as a good dog," he once wrote, "but we can all try." Yes, Mark Twain may not have loved dogs quite as much as he loved cats, but he wrote a book about a dog—something he never did for a cat. In fact, his "good dog" remark comes from his inscription in a copy of that book, *A Dog's Tale*, that he gave to an animal rights organization he supported.

A DOG'S TALE

·

MARK TWAIN

A Dog's Tale, *1904, cover*

Mark Twain was surrounded by cats throughout his life, but dogs were also always nearby, from his early boyhood to the last day of his life, when he shared his bedroom with a dog. Several dogs—real and imaginary—played notable roles in his career as an author. For example, if it weren't for a forlorn mutt in Nevada, the world might never have known the name "Mark Twain." According to a story published after he died, one day in 1864, when he was standing on a corner in Virginia City, Nevada, "a mangy dog came up and rubbed its itching side against [his] leg." Mark Twain "merely looked down and drawled out: 'Well, if I've become a scratching post for Steve Gillis's dogs, I'd better hit the trail.'" Shortly afterward, he was on his way to California, where he would write the jumping frog story that launched him on the path to world fame. Incidentally, that story about a remarkable frog named Dan'l Webster also tells about an even more remarkable dog named after another famous American, Andrew Jackson (see chapter 13).

Here's something else few people know: Not only did Mark Twain write a book about a dog, but another dog was indirectly responsible for the title of his 1894 novel *Pudd'nhead Wilson*. What Mark Twain liked least about dogs was their tendency to yelp and bark. In his novel, a disagreeably yelping and snarling dog prompts the young lawyer David Wilson to say something that earns him the unfortunate nickname that gives the novel its title (see chapter 26).

Andrew Jackson and the yelping *Pudd'nhead Wilson* dog are among the many imaginary dogs you will meet in this book, but you will also meet many real dogs that Mark Twain encountered in his life, as well as a few dogs he never knew that were named after him. One of the most moving stories about real dogs comes from an essay Mark Twain wrote about the sudden death of his youngest daughter, Jean, in 1909—only four months before his own death. The last thing he wrote for publication, that essay also contains his last writing about an animal—a tribute to Jean's German shepherd, Fix, the dog that was to share his bedroom through his last months (see chapter 12).

Speaking of real dogs, one of the fun things about reading Mark Twain's dog stories is wondering how much of what he wrote was true. As an heir to the southwestern tradition of the tall tale, he was prone to embellish and exaggerate, muddying the line between truth and fiction in his writings. Even scholars aren't always sure whether to call a book like *Roughing It*, his 1872 account of his experiences in the Far West, fiction or nonfiction. Some of his readers had the same problem. In 1880, a cheese merchant in New York told Mark Twain that he had read *Roughing It* and others of his books and wanted "to know . . . by what rule a fellow can infallibly judge when you are lying and when you are telling the truth." He then suggested that Mark Twain's next book "be published with the truth printed in italics." Mark Twain laughed off that suggestion with this comment: "Ha!—ha! . . . captured another idiot," but that didn't answer the reader's question.

It might help if the present volume were to print true statements in italics, but that would require knowing which statements *are* true. Readers are invited to draw their own conclusions. Perhaps it will help you get started to know that Mark Twain's claim that an uncle of his "used to own a dog that was descended from the dog that was in the Ark" probably was not true. (He made that claim in his 1907 book *Christian Science*, which contains one or two other claims of dubious veracity.) On the other hand, you might simply ignore such questions and instead concentrate on enjoying the stories, each of which has its own unique fascination.

The Clemens family on the porch of their Hartford home with the family dog Flash. From left to right: Livy, Clara, Jean, Sam, and Susy. COURTESY OF THE MARK TWAIN PROJECT, THE BANCROFT LIBRARY, UNIVERSITY OF CALIFORNIA, BERKELEY

PART I.

MARK TWAIN IN THE COMPANY OF DOGS

Mark Twain was never far from dogs throughout his life. Pets and strays ran loose in his hometown of Hannibal, Missouri, and he spent most of his youthful summers at his uncle's nearby Florida, Missouri, farm, which swarmed with hunting dogs. During his adult years, he encountered innumerable dogs on his extensive travels along the Mississippi River, in the Far West and Hawaii, and in the many foreign countries he visited. Meanwhile, he raised a family in Hartford, Connecticut, that generally had at least one dog—usually the special pet of his youngest daughter, Jean—and his family regularly summered at his sister-in-law's farm in Elmira, New York, where more dogs roamed.

1.

HUNTING DOGS

———————

Mark Twain's autobiography, which has been published in numer-
ous forms, is rich in poignant memories of his youth. He grew up
in the riverside Missouri town of Hannibal but spent most of his
summers at the Florida, Missouri, farm of his uncle John Quarles.
His warm recollections of the farm's hound dogs would later find
fictional expression in his writings about Tom Sawyer and Huck-
leberry Finn.

———————

I remember the 'coon and 'possum hunts, nights, with the
negroes, and the long marches through the black gloom
of the woods, and the excitement which fired everybody
when the distant bay of an experienced dog announced that
the game was treed; then the wild scramblings and stumblings
through briars and bushes and over roots to get to the spot;
then the lighting of a fire and the felling of the tree, the joyful

Edmund Henry Osthaus, "Afield." COURTESY LIBRARY OF CONGRESS

frenzy of the dogs and the negroes, and the weird picture it all made in the red glare—I remember it all well, and the delight that every one got out of it, except the 'coon.

I remember the pigeon seasons, when the birds would come in millions, and cover the trees, and by their weight break down the branches. They were clubbed to death with sticks; guns were not necessary, and were not used. I remember the squirrel hunts, and the prairie-chicken hunts, and the wild-turkey hunts, and all that; and how we turned out, mornings, while it was still dark, to go on these expeditions, and how chilly and dismal it was, and how often I regretted that I was well enough to go. A toot on a tin horn brought twice as many dogs as were needed, and in their happiness they raced and scampered about, and knocked small people down, and made no end of unnecessary noise. At the word, they vanished away toward the woods, and we drifted silently after them in the melancholy gloom. But presently the gray dawn stole over the world, the birds piped up, then the sun rose and poured light and comfort all around, everything was fresh and dewy and fragrant, and life was a boon again. After three hours of tramping we arrived back wholesomely tired, overladen with game, very hungry, and just in time for breakfast.

2.

A VASTLY FUNNY ANECDOTE
ABOUT A DOG

———————••••••———————

Mark Twain's 1883 book Life on the Mississippi *contains his poignant memoir of his cub steamboat piloting days during the late 1850s. Among the memorable river characters the book describes was the overbearing pilot William Brown—whose murder the book's young cub fantasizes about every night. Among Brown's numerous irritating quirks was a memory so prodigious that it got in the way of his finishing stories, as this next passage demonstrates. Brown, incidentally, may have been an inspiration for the immortal Jim Blaine of "Story of the Old Ram" fame (see chapter 18).*

———————••••••———————

And so on, by the hour, the man's tongue would go. He could *not* forget any thing. It was simply impossible. The most trivial details remained as distinct and

The cub pilot meeting the surly Mr. Brown. JOHN J. HARLEY, *LIFE ON THE MISSISSIPPI*, 1883, PAGE 219

luminous in his head, after they had lain there for years, as the most memorable events. . . .

Such a memory as that is a great misfortune. To it, all occurrences are of the same size. Its possessor cannot distinguish an interesting circumstance from an uninteresting one.

As a talker, he is bound to clog his narrative with tiresome details and make himself an insufferable bore. Moreover, he cannot stick to his subject. He picks up every little grain of memory he discerns in his way, and so is led aside. Mr. Brown would start out with the honest intention of telling you a vastly funny anecdote about a dog. He would be "so full of laugh" that he could hardly begin; then his memory would start with the dog's breed and personal appearance; drift into a history of his owner; of his owner's family, with descriptions of weddings and burials that had occurred in it, together with recitals of congratulatory verses and obituary poetry provoked by the same; then this memory would recollect that one of these events occurred during the celebrated "hard winter" of such and such a year, and a minute description of that winter would follow, along with the names of people who were frozen to death, and statistics showing the high figures which pork and hay went up to. Pork and hay would suggest corn and fodder; corn and fodder would suggest cows and horses; cows and horses would suggest the circus and certain celebrated bare-back riders; the transition from the circus to the menagerie was easy and natural; from the elephant to equatorial Africa was but a step; then of course the heathen savages would suggest religion; and at the end of three or four hours' tedious jaw, the watch would change, and Brown would go out of the pilot-house muttering extracts from sermons he had heard years before about the efficacy of prayer as a means of grace. And the original first mention would be all you had learned about that dog, after all this waiting and hungering.

3.

NO PUPPYISH LEVITY

After piloting steamboats on the Mississippi for four years, Mark Twain went to Nevada, became a newspaper reporter, and adopted his famous pen name. In 1864, he relocated to San Francisco, California, and reported for the Daily Morning Call. *At that time, the booming city was overrun by homeless dogs that were targets of anti-stray laws and occasional extermination campaigns. Two strays, however, had become so famous for their prowess in killing rats—which were also overrunning the city—they were exempted from government anti-dog efforts. The dog known as Bummer was of Newfoundland extraction. His devoted partner, Lazarus, was of less certain pedigree. In October 1863, before Mark Twain arrived, Lazarus had been killed in myste-rious circumstances, leaving Bummer to find a new partner. It didn't take Mark Twain long to find something to write about these dogs, whose fame would eventually inspire several books.*

Imaginative illustration of Bummer and Lazarus begging food from another notorious San Francisco figure, Norton I—the self-styled "Emperor of the United States." EDWARD JUMP, WIKIMEDIA

The lamented Lazarus departed this life about a year ago, and from that time until recently poor Bummer has mourned the loss of his faithful friend in solitude, scorning the sympathy and companionship of his race with that stately reserve and exclusiveness which has always distinguished him since he became a citizen of San Francisco. But, for several weeks past, we have observed a vagrant black puppy has taken up with him, and attends him in his promenades, bums with him at the restaurants, and watches over his slumbers as unremittingly as did the sainted Lazarus of other days. Whether that puppy really feels an unselfish affection for Bummer, or whether he is actuated by unworthy motives, and goes with him merely to ring in on the eating houses through his popularity at such establishments, or whether he is one of those fawning sycophants that fasten upon the world's heroes in order that they may be glorified by the reflected light of greatness, we can not yet determine. We only know that he hangs around Bummer, and snarls at intruders upon his repose, and looks proud and happy when the old dog condescends to notice him. He ventures upon no puppyish levity in the presence of his prince, and essays no unbecoming familiarity, but in all respects conducts himself with the respectful decorum which such a puppy so situated should display. Consequently, in time, he may grow into high favor.

4.

EXIT BUMMER

———••◆••———

A year after eulogizing the late lamented Lazarus, Mark Twain wrote an obituary for Lazarus's former partner, Bummer, for the Virginia City Territorial Enterprise. This text comes from the reprinted article in San Francisco's Californian, whose editor, Bret Harte, introduces it.

———••◆••———

As we have devoted but little space to an event which has filled our local contemporaries with as much sorrow (judging from the columns of lamentations it has called forth) as would the decease of the best biped in the city, we give "Mark Twain's" view of the occurrence as recorded in the *Enterprise* of the 8th. Strangely enough, Mark, who can't stand "ballad infliction" seems to think there has not been quite enough of "Bummer":

THE DAMON AND PYTHIAS OF SAN FRANCISCO.

THEIR LIVES AND THEIR DEATHS. THEIR SEPARATION AND THEIR FINAL
REUNION IN THE DOG STAR—THE PLACE WHERE GOOD DOGS GO.

Rats gather to celebrate the death of San Francisco's most notorious rat-killer. EDWARD
JUMP, WIKIMEDIA

The old vagrant "Bummer" is really dead at last; and
although he was always more respected than his obsequious
vassal, the dog "Lazarus," his exit has not made half as much
stir in the newspaper world as signalised the departure of
the latter. I think it is because he died a natural death: died
with friends around him to smooth his pillow and wipe the
death-damps from his brow, and receive his last words of love
and resignation; because he died full of years, and honor, and

disease, and fleas. He was permitted to die a natural death, as I have said, but poor Lazarus "died with his boots on"—which is to say, he lost his life by violence; he gave up the ghost mysteriously, at dead of night, with none to cheer his last moments or soothe his dying pains. So the murdered dog was canonized in the newspapers, his shortcomings excused and his virtues heralded to the world; but his superior, parting with his life in the fullness of time, and in the due course of nature, sinks as quietly as might the mangiest cur among us. Well, let him go. In earlier days he was courted and caressed; but latterly he has lost his comeliness—his dignity had given place to a want of self-respect, which allowed him to practice mean deceptions to regain for a moment that sympathy and notice which had become necessary to his very existence, and it was evident to all that the dog had had his day; his great popularity was gone forever. In fact, Bummer should have died sooner: there was a time when his death would have left a lasting legacy of fame to his name. Now, however, he will be forgotten in a few days. Bummer's skin is to be stuffed and placed with that of Lazarus.

———••———•———••———

The above eulogy may not have been Mark Twain's last word on Bummer. This next article appeared in the San Francisco Dramatic Chronicle *on November 11, 1865. It is not entirely certain Mark Twain himself wrote it, but it resembles his style and reflects his disdain for his then-former employer, the* Morning Call. *(The stuffed bodies of Lazarus and Bummer, incidentally, were stored in the forerunner of San Francisco's M. H. de Young Memorial*

Museum until they were destroyed in 1910—the year of Mark Twain's death.)

———————————

Good kindly-hearted Bummer, the pet of the public, lies a corpse, and now, while the sorrow-stricken people bemoan his loss, the horrid, fiendish little *Call* publishes a paragraph which commences thus: "Jump upon Bummer." You'd like to jump upon him now he's dead, would you? You daren't do it while he was alive. "Jump upon Bummer!"—Isn't this pretty advice to give to people who loved and respected him while alive, and now mourn his loss. We are not in favor of mob law, but—could it cause any surprise if an enraged populace demolished the office of the paper which dared to say "Jump upon Bummer." The remainder of the paragraph may possibly afford an explanation of the reasons the cowardly little *Call* has for saying, "Jump upon Bummer," but we are sure that nothing can extenuate the barbarity of such advice. When we saw that first line it was enough for us—we threw down the *Call* in disgust and jumped upon that. We read no further; we hope we are not yet so hard up for reading matter as to be driven to read the local items of the *Call*.

5.

GENERAL MILES AND THE DOG

———————◆———————

Mark Twain told this story about the distinguished Civil War general Nelson Appleton Miles several times throughout his life. This version comes from a section of his autobiography he dictated in October 1907. It recalls an incident that supposedly occurred in 1867, while he was living in Washington, DC, struggling to earn a living as a journalist and writing his first major book, The Innocents Abroad. *He and his friend William Clinton were living on a tight budget of twenty-four dollars a week.*

———————◆———————

Clinton was one of the dearest and loveliest human beings I have ever known, and we led a charmed existence together, in a contentment which knew no bounds. Clinton was refined by nature and breeding; he was a gentleman by nature and breeding; he was highly educated; he was of a beautiful spirit; he was pure in heart and speech. He was a Scotchman, and a Presbyterian; a Presbyterian of the old and genuine school, being honest and sincere in his religion, and loving it, and finding serenity and peace in it. He hadn't a vice—unless a large and grateful sympathy with Scotch whiskey may be called by that name. I didn't regard it as a vice, because he was a Scotchman, and Scotch whiskey to a Scotchman is as innocent as milk is to the rest of the human race. In Clinton's case it was a virtue, and not an economical one. Twenty-four dollars a week would really have been riches to us if we hadn't had to support that jug; because of the jug we were always sailing pretty close to the wind, and any tardiness in the arrival of any part of our income was sure to cause us some inconvenience.

I remember a time when a shortage occurred; we had to have three dollars, and we had to have it before the close of the day. I don't know now how we happened to want all that money at one time; I only know we had to have it. Clinton told me to go out and find it—and he said he would also go out and see what he could do. He didn't seem to have any doubt that we would succeed, but I knew that that was his religion working in him; I hadn't the same confidence; I hadn't any idea where to turn to raise all that bullion, and I said so. I think he was ashamed of me, privately, because of my weak faith. He told me to give myself no uneasiness, no concern; and said in a simple, confident, and unquestioning way, "the Lord will provide." I saw that he fully believed the Lord would provide, but it seemed to me that if he had had my experience—

But never mind that; before he was done with me his strong faith had had its influence, and I went forth from the place almost convinced that the Lord really would provide.

I wandered around the streets for an hour, trying to think up some way to get that money, but nothing suggested itself. At last I lounged into the big lobby of the Ebbitt House, which was then a new hotel, and sat down. Presently a dog came loafing along. He paused, glanced up at me and said, with his eyes, "Are you friendly?" I answered, with my eyes, that I was. He gave his tail a grateful little wag and came forward and rested his jaw on my knee and lifted his brown eyes to my face in a winningly affectionate way. He was a lovely creature—as beautiful as a girl, and he was made all of silk and velvet. I stroked his smooth brown head and fondled his drooping ears, and we were a pair of lovers right away. Pretty soon Brigadier-General Miles, the hero of the land, came strolling by in his blue and gold splendors, with everybody's admiring gaze upon him. He saw the dog and stopped, and there was a light in his eye which showed that he had a warm place in his heart for dogs like this gracious creature; then he came forward and patted the dog and said,

"He is very fine—he is a wonder; would you sell him?"

I was greatly moved; it seemed a marvellous thing to me, the way Clinton's prediction had come true. I said, "Yes."

The General said, "What do you ask for him?"

"Three dollars."

The General was manifestly surprised. He said, "Three dollars? Only three dollars? Why, that dog is a most uncommon dog; he can't possibly be worth less than fifty. If he were mine, I wouldn't take a hundred for him. I'm afraid you are not aware of his value. Reconsider your price if you like, I don't wish to wrong you."

But if he had known me he would have known that I was no more capable of wronging him than he was of wronging me. I responded with the same quiet decision as before, "No—three dollars. That is his price."

"Very well, since you insist upon it," said the General, and he gave me three dollars and led the dog away, and disappeared up-stairs.

In about ten minutes a gentle-faced middle-aged gentleman came along, and began to look around here and there and under tables and everywhere, and I said to him, "Is it a dog you are looking for?"

His face was sad, before, and troubled; but it lit up gladly now, and he answered, "Yes—have you seen him?"

"Yes," I said, "he was here a minute ago, and I saw him follow a gentleman away. I think I could find him for you if you would like me to try."

I have seldom seen a person look so grateful—and there was gratitude in his voice, too, when he conceded that he would like me to try. I said I would do it with great pleasure, but that as it might take a little time I hoped he would not mind paying me something for my trouble. He said he would do it most gladly—repeating that phrase "most gladly"—and asked me how much. I said—"Three dollars."

He looked surprised, and said, "Dear me, it is nothing! I will pay you ten, quite willingly."

But I said, "No, three is the price"—and I started for the stairs without waiting for any further argument, for Clinton had said that that was the amount that the Lord would provide,

EMLEN MCCONNELL, *BOSTON SUNDAY POST MAGAZINE*, SEPTEMBER 13, 1908

and it seemed to me that it would be sacrilegious to take a penny more than was promised.

I got the number of the General's room from the office-clerk, as I passed by his wicket, and when I reached the room I found the General there caressing his dog, and quite happy. I said, "I am sorry, but I have to take the dog again."

He seemed very much surprised, and said, "Take him again? Why, he is my dog; you sold him to me, and at your own price."

"Yes," I said, "it is true—but I have to have him, because the man wants him again."

"What man?"

"The man that owns him; he wasn't my dog."

The General looked even more surprised than before, and for a moment he couldn't seem to find his voice; then he said, "Do you mean to tell me that you were selling another man's dog—and knew it?"

"Yes, I knew it wasn't my dog."

"Then why did you sell him?"

I said, "Well, that is a curious question to ask. I sold him because you wanted him. You offered to buy the dog; you can't deny that. I was not anxious to sell him—I had not even thought of selling him, but it seemed to me that if it could be any accommodation to you—"

He broke me off in the middle, and said, "*Accommodation to me?* It is the most extraordinary spirit of accommodation I have ever heard of—the idea of your selling a dog that didn't belong to you—"

I broke him off there, and said, "There is no relevancy about this kind of argument; you said yourself that the dog was probably worth a hundred dollars, I only asked you three; was there anything unfair about that? You offered to pay more, you know you did. I only asked you three; you can't deny it."

"Oh, what in the world has that to do with it! The crux of the matter is that you didn't own the dog—can't you see that? You seem to think that there is no impropriety in selling property that isn't yours provided you sell it cheap. Now, then—"

I said, "Please don't argue about it any more. You can't get around the fact that the price was perfectly fair, perfectly reasonable—considering that I didn't own the dog—and so arguing about it is only a waste of words. I have to have him back again because the man wants him; don't you see that I haven't any choice in the matter? Put yourself in my place. Suppose you had sold a dog that didn't belong to you; suppose you—"

"Oh," he said, "don't muddle my brains any more with your idiotic reasonings! Take him along, and give me a rest."

So I paid back the three dollars and led the dog down-stairs and passed him over to his owner, and collected three for my trouble.

I went away then with a good conscience, because I had acted honorably; I never could have used the three that I sold the dog for, because it was not rightly my own, but the three I got for restoring him to his rightful owner was righteously and properly mine, because I had earned it. That man might never have gotten that dog back at all, if it hadn't been for me. My principles have remained to this day what they were then. I was always honest; I know I can never be otherwise. It is as I said in the beginning—I was never able to persuade myself to use money which I had acquired in questionable ways.

Now, then, that is the tale. Some of it is true.

Mark Twain told this story, which has been published in several slightly different versions, on several public occasions, most memorably, perhaps, in Bermuda in 1908. According to Elizabeth

Wallace's 1913 book, Mark Twain and the Happy Island, *Mark Twain was a past master of keeping a straight face while speaking, "no matter how excruciatingly absurd the story was." On that Bermuda occasion, however, "when he reached the climax of the story, he suddenly broke down and laughed, laughed so hard that for a minute he could not go on. And the audience shook with mirth because of the unexpectedness of it."*

———•••◆•••———

6.

THE TERRIER AND
THE OYSTER CRACKERS

———————•———————

By the late 1870s, Mark Twain was famous as the author of The
Innocents Abroad, Roughing It, The Adventures of Tom
Sawyer *and other works. He was married, with children, and living
in a magnificent custom-built home in Hartford, Connecticut. The
1878 story from the* New York Sun *that follows here describes what
appears to have been a wholly imaginary interview with him.*

For the record: Mark Twain never worked for the Hartford
Courant *or owned a terrier dog like the one described in the story.
Moreover, Russia was fighting the Turkish-ruled Ottoman Empire
in 1877–1878, but Great Britain did not get directly involved. Jose-
phus Cook, incidentally, was a Boston evangelical lecturer then
frequently in the news.*

———————•———————

The Clemens family's Hartford home. COURTESY LIBRARY OF CONGRESS

HARTFORD, Jan. 25.—Wishing to obtain Mark Twain's views on the probability of a war between England and Russia, I went to the office of the *Courant* expecting to find him at his desk. To my surprise, I was told that he had not been in the office for near a fortnight. Then I called at the door of his astonishing residence in the outskirts of the city. The domestic informed me that I would find Mr. Clemens in the back yard. When I approached the celebrated humorist he was sitting on an inverted washtub, trying to teach a frowsy little terrier to catch crackers in its mouth. Twain had his hat full of oyster crackers. The dog stood on its hind legs and snapped with much perseverance, but with only a moderate degree of skill, at the bits tossed by the master. To set a good example, Twain tossed every third or fourth cracker up in the air, catching it in his own mouth as it descended, and never missing. I complimented him upon his surprising dexterity.

"Oh," said he, carelessly, "a great deal can be accomplished by practice. Here Jo!"

"Is your dog named Joseph?"

"I call him Jo Cook because I can't quite understand him. There are depths in that dog's nature that I haven't fathomed."

"Don't you consider that you are neglecting your professional duties? They told me at the office that you hadn't been seen there for a fortnight. No journalist can expect to give his paper a consistent tone when he indulges in such protracted absences. Matters at Washington are interesting just now, and the Eastern question has assumed a new and critical phase; and yet here you are, out in the back yard, tossing oyster crackers to a small dog. I ask you, sincerely as a friend, can you hope to succeed as an editor if you continue to act thus?"

"Young fellow," said Clemens, with great seriousness of manner, "did you swallow that yarn?" "Didn't I tell you," said Twain, after a brief pause—"Didn't I tell you just as you were getting up (at last!) to go, that the story was told, not for publication, but merely as a guarantee of good faith?"

"Yes, you told me that, but at the same time you took the trouble to wink hard with your left eye, and nobody knows better than yourself the significance of a wink under such circumstances."

7.

NO DOG LEFT BEHIND

In 1882, Mark Twain revisited the Mississippi River to gather material for Life on the Mississippi. *While cruising down the river south of Memphis, Tennessee, he observed many recently emancipated slave families traveling on steamboats to find employment and to satisfy their long-suppressed desire to travel. Mark Twain had immense respect for African Americans. What he says here about their children needn't be taken seriously.*

We were getting down now into the migrating negro region. These poor people could never travel when they were slaves; so they make up for the privation now. They stay on a plantation till the desire to travel seizes them; then they pack up, hail a steamboat, and clear out. Not for any particular place; no, nearly any place will answer; they only want to be moving. The amount of money

A. B. SHUTE, *LIFE ON THE MISSISSIPPI*, 1883, PAGE 327

on hand will answer the rest of the conundrum for them. If it will take them fifty miles, very well; let it be fifty. If not, a shorter flight will do.

During a couple of days, we frequently answered these hails. Sometimes there was a group of high-water-stained, tumble-down cabins, populous with colored folk, and no whites visible; with grassless patches of dry ground here and there; a few felled trees, with skeleton cattle, mules, and horses, eating the leaves and gnawing the bark—no other food for them in the flood-wasted land. Sometimes there was a single lonely landing-cabin; near it the colored family that had hailed us; little and big, old and young, roosting on the scant pile of household goods; these consisting of a rusty gun, some bedticks, chests, tinware, stools, a crippled looking-glass, a venerable arm-chair, and six or eight base-born and spiritless yellow curs, attached to the family by strings. They must have their dogs; can't go without their dogs. Yet the dogs are never willing; they always object; so, one after another, in ridiculous procession, they are dragged aboard; all four feet braced and sliding along the stage, head likely to be pulled off; but the tugger marching determinedly forward, bending to his work, with the rope over his shoulder for better purchase. Sometimes a child is forgotten and left on the bank; but never a dog.

8.

BICYCLES VS. DOGS

During the early 1880s, Mark Twain, along with his friend and Hartford neighbor Joseph Twichell, took bicycle-riding lessons. His posthumously published account of their experience highlights the complications dogs added to cycling.

There was a row of low stepping-stones across one end of the street, a measured yard apart. Even after I got so I could steer pretty fairly I was so afraid of those stones that I always hit them. They gave me the worst falls I ever got in that street, except those which I got from dogs. I have seen it stated that no expert is quick enough to run over a dog; that a dog is always able to skip out of his way. I think that that may be true: but I think that the reason he couldn't run over the dog was because he was trying to. I did not try to run over any dog. But I ran over every dog that came along. I think

A. B. Frost, "What Happened?" c. 1897, COURTESY, LIBRARY OF CONGRESS.
DOG AND MARK TWAIN'S FACE HAVE BEEN ADDED.

it makes a great deal of difference. If you try to run over the dog he knows how to calculate, but if you are trying to miss him he does not know how to calculate, and is liable to jump the wrong way every time. It was always so in my experience. Even when I could not hit a wagon I could hit a dog that came to see me practice. They all liked to see me practice, and they all came, for there was very little going on in our neighborhood to entertain a dog. It took time to learn to miss a dog, but I achieved even that. . . .

Get a bicycle. You will not regret it, if you live.

9.

LIVELY TIMES FOR THE FAMILY CATS

In 1887, Mark Twain wrote a letter to his mother from his sister-in-law's Elmira, New York, farm, where his family spent most of their summers. It describes the seventh birthday of the family's youngest daughter, Jean. As the family "expert on animals," Jean would also become the family's chief admirer of dogs. Despite her youth, she probably had a leading role in the incident Mark Twain describes here.

We have put in this whole Sunday forenoon teaching the new dog to let the cats alone, & it has been uncommonly lively for those 5 cats. They have spent the most of the time in the trees, swearing. He is the alertest dog that ever was; nothing escapes his observation; & as to movement, he makes a white streak through the air 30 yards long when he is getting started; after that he is invisible.

10.

ENTERTAINING WATCH DOGS

———————◆———————

In June 1908, Mark Twain settled into his last home, a custom-built mansion outside Redding, Connecticut. In September, two burglars invaded his home. The timely appearance of Mark Twain's secretary scared them off with only a bundle of silverware, but they were soon caught and later served prison sentences for their crime. Although Mark Twain was upset by the incident, which triggered the resignations of his entire domestic staff, his public reaction was flippant. A little later, he helped found Redding's first public library by issuing the appeal that follows below.

———————◆———————

I am going to help build that library with contributions— from my visitors. Every male guest who comes to my house will have to contribute a dollar or go away without his baggage. If those burglars that broke into my house recently had done that they would have been happier now, or

Mark Twain posing with a gun outside his Stormfield residence shortly after the burglary. COURTESY OF THE MARK TWAIN PROJECT, THE BANCROFT LIBRARY, UNIVERSITY OF CALIFORNIA, BERKELEY

if they'd have broken into this library they would have read a few books and led a better life. Now they are in jail, and if they keep on they will go to Congress. When a person starts downhill you can never tell where he's going to stop. I am sorry for those burglars. They got nothing that they wanted and scared away most of my servants. Now we are putting in a burglar-alarm instead of a dog. Some advised the dog, but it costs even more to entertain a dog than a burglar. I am having the ground electrified, so that for a mile around any one who puts his foot across the line sets off an alarm that will be heard in Europe.

———————

Mark Twain was actually a little inconsistent on the subject of watchdogs. The morning after the burglary, he wrote to a young friend named Margaret Blackmer: "Burglars in the house after midnight this morning. They are on their way to jail this afternoon. We are buying a couple of bulldogs & hoping they will call again." A day or two later, he wrote to journalist Melville E. Stone, "No. I can get burglars here at club rates and they pay their own fare. Can you lend me a dog? I want one that will leave strawberries and cream to eat burglar."

———————

11.

MARK TWAIN AND
THE TRICK DOG

———————•———————

By the turn of the twentieth century, Mark Twain had one of the
most recognizable faces on the planet. His flowing white hair and
the brilliantly white suits he began wearing around 1906 made him
stand out in any crowd—a fact that wasn't entirely accidental. In
fact, he so loved being the center of public attention we can only
wonder what he thought of the dog in this 1909 Manhattan news
item.

———————•———————

The sidewalks of the avenue were thronged. Moving
at a leisurely pace a continuous stream of pedestrians
threw a brilliant ribbon of calm as far as the eye could
reach. At Forty-Fourth street, at the most crowded hour, a
small knot of persons had gathered intent upon the same
object. A woman who was just behind the group observed the

Early twentieth-century Manhattan street scene. COURTESY LIBRARY OF CONGRESS

cause of this little gathering as she supposed, and turning to her companion:

"How gratifying," she said. "See, there is Mark Twain waiting for a bus, and so many have stopped to look at him. He has his back to them and doesn't know a thing about it. Quite a tribute, isn't it?"

But by this time the women were abreast of the group. The real object of interest was something entirely different. Standing back of Mark Twain was a woman, and beside her a French poodle sitting upright, his mistress' purse held tightly in his mouth. Not one of the group had recognized the distinguished author nor had a moment for him in the absorption of watching the trick dog.

12.

THE LAST FAMILY DOG

———————◆———————

One of Mark Twain's most heartbreaking experiences occurred near the end of his life when his twenty-nine-year-old daughter, Jean, died on Christmas Eve 1909—only a few months before his own death. Epilepsy had long made Jean's health fragile, but the suddenness of her death was a shocking blow, especially as she had been Mark Twain's only relative still living with him. Immediately after Jean died, he began writing a lament that would reveal how her pet dog, Fix, comforted him.

———————◆———————

Last night Jean, all flushed with splendid health, and I the same, from the wholesome effects of my Bermuda holiday, strolled hand in hand from the dinner-table and sat down in the library and chatted, and planned, and discussed, cheerily and happily (and how unsuspectingly!)—until nine—which is late for us—then went upstairs, Jean's friendly

No photo of Jean with her German shepherd Fix has been found. This photo shows Jean (center) in 1906 with her St. Bernard Prosper, her father (right), and his secretary, Isabel Lyon (left). COURTESY OF KEVIN MAC DONNELL, AUSTIN, TEXAS

German dog following. At my door Jean said, "I can't kiss you good night, father: I have a cold, and you could catch it." I bent and kissed her hand. She was moved—I saw it in her eyes—and she impulsively kissed my hand in return. Then with the usual gay "Sleep well, dear!" from both, we parted.

At half past seven this morning I woke, and heard voices outside my door. I said to myself, "Jean is starting on her usual horseback flight to the station for the mail." Then Katy [a family servant] entered, stood quaking and gasping at my bedside a moment, then found her tongue:

"MISS JEAN IS DEAD!"

Possibly I know now what the soldier feels when a bullet crashes through his heart.

In her bathroom there she lay, the fair young creature, stretched upon the floor and covered with a sheet. And looking so placid, so natural, and as if asleep. We knew what had happened. She was an epileptic: she had been seized with a convulsion and heart failure in her bath. The doctor had to come several miles. His efforts, like our previous ones, failed to bring her back to life. . . .

Her dog has been wandering about the grounds today, comradeless and forlorn. I have seen him from the windows. She got him from Germany. He has tall ears and looks exactly like a wolf. He was educated in Germany, and knows no language but the German. Jean gave him no orders save in that tongue. And so when the burglar-alarm made a fierce clamor at midnight a fortnight ago, the butler, who is French and knows no German, tried in vain to interest the dog in the supposed burglar. Jean wrote me, to Bermuda, about the incident. It was the last letter I was ever to receive from her bright head and her competent hand. The dog will not be neglected.

There was never a kinder heart than Jean's. From her childhood up she always spent the most of her allowance on charities of one kind or another. After she became secretary and had her income doubled she spent her money upon these things with a free hand. Mine too, I am glad and grateful to say.

She was a loyal friend to all animals, and she loved them all, birds, beasts, and everything—even snakes—an inheritance from me. She knew all the birds; she was high up in that lore.

She became a member of various humane societies when she was still a little girl—both here and abroad—and she remained an active member to the last. She founded two or three societies for the protection of animals, here and in Europe. . . .

About three in the morning, while wandering about the house in the deep silences, as one does in times like these, when there is a dumb sense that something has been lost that will never be found again, yet must be sought, if only for the employment the useless seeking gives, I came upon Jean's dog in the hall downstairs, and noted that he did not spring to greet me, according to his hospitable habit, but came slow and sorrowfully; also I remembered that he had not visited Jean's apartment since the tragedy. Poor fellow, did he know? I think so. Always when Jean was abroad in the open he was with her; always when she was in the house he was with her, in the night as well as in the day. Her parlor was his bedroom. Whenever I happened upon him on the ground floor he always followed me about, and when I went upstairs he went too—in a tumultuous gallop. But now it was different: after patting him a little I went to the library—he remained behind; when I went upstairs he did not follow me, save with his wistful eyes. He has wonderful eyes—big, and kind, and eloquent. He can talk with them. He is a beautiful creature, and is of the breed of the New York police-dogs. I do not like dogs, because they bark when there is no occasion for it; but I have liked this one from the beginning, because he belonged to Jean, and because he never barks except when there is occasion—which is not oftener than twice a week. . . .

They told me the first mourner to come was the dog. He came uninvited, and stood up on his hind legs and rested his fore paws upon the trestle, and took a last long look at the face that was so dear to him, then went his way as silently as he had come. HE KNOWS. . . .

DECEMBER 26TH. The dog came to see me at eight o'clock this morning. He was very affectionate, poor orphan! My room will be his quarters hereafter.

Four days before Mark Twain died, his daughter Clara and her husband, Ossip Gabrilowitsch, arrived at Stormfield. They remained there until after Clara's daughter, Nina, was born—and then returned to Europe. By then, Ossip had bonded with Fix, whom they took with them. Unfortunately, in Munich, Germany, Fix ran loose onto a street and was struck by a car. Diligent care in a hospital failed to save him, and he died with his head in Ossip's lap.

FRED STROTHMANN, *THE JUMPING FROG*, 1903, PAGE 18

PART II.

---·---

UNCOMMON CANINES

Always a perceptive observer of nature, Mark Twain wrote at length about interesting and unusual animals, especially in his travel books. Not surprisingly, he found more than a few dogs during his world travels worthy of special praise. Some will appear later in the book. This section describes the most exceptional animals, some of whom were even real.

13.

A DOG WITH GENIUS IN HIM

———•—•———

Mark Twain's name is indelibly associated with a certain frog he celebrated early in his writing career. His famous sketch about that frog is actually principally about its owner, Jim Smiley, a Calaveras County mining camp resident during California's gold rush days. An obsessive and wily gambler, Smiley is always ready to bet on anything. He is eventually outslickered, however, when an even wilier stranger secretly fills his champion frog full of quail-shot to win a jumping contest. The sketch made Smiley's frog justly famous, but the frog wasn't Smiley's only animal prodigy.

———•—•———

And he had a little small bull-pup, that to look at him you'd think he wan't worth a cent but to set around and look ornery and lay for a chance to steal something. But as soon as money was up on him he was a different

FRED STROTHMANN, *THE JUMPING FROG*, 1903, PAGE 18

dog; his under-jaw'd begin to stick out like the fo'castle of a steamboat, and his teeth would uncover and shine like the furnaces. And a dog might tackle him and bully-rag him and bite him and throw him over his shoulder two or three times, and Andrew Jackson—which was the name of the pup—Andrew Jackson would never let on but what *he* was satisfied, and hadn't expected nothing else—and the bets being doubled and doubled on the other side all the time, till the money was all up; and then all of a sudden he would grab that other dog jest by the j'int of his hind leg and freeze to it—not chaw, you understand, but only just grip and hang on till they throwed up the sponge, if it was a year. Smiley always come out winner on that pup, till he harnessed a dog once that didn't have no hind legs, because they'd been sawed off in a circular saw, and when the thing had gone along far enough, and the money was all up, and he come to make a snatch for his pet holt, he see in a minute how he'd been imposed on, and how the other dog had him in the door, so to speak, and he 'peared surprised, and then he looked sorter discouraged-like, and didn't try no more to win the fight, and so he got shucked out bad. He give Smiley a look, as much as to say his heart was broke, and it was *his* fault, for putting up a dog that hadn't no hind legs for him to take holt of, which was his main dependence in a fight, and then he limped off a piece and laid down and died. It was a good pup, was that Andrew Jackson, and would have made a name for hisself if he'd lived, for the stuff was in him and he had genius—I know it, because he hadn't no opportunities to speak of, and it don't stand to reason that a dog could make such a fight as he could under them circumstances, if he hadn't no talent. It always makes me feel sorry when I think of that last fight of his'n, and the way it turned out.

14.

A LIVING, BREATHING ALLEGORY OF WANT

———••—•—••———

A distant relative of the domestic dog that Mark Twain admired was the North American coyote, which he saw in abundance in the West during the early 1860s. Roughing It, *his 1872 book about his years in the West, describes his first encounter with a coyote in what is now the state of Nebraska. This anecdote also includes a memorable encounter with a more ordinary dog.*

———••—•—••———

Along about an hour after breakfast we saw the first prairie-dog villages, the first antelope, and the first wolf. If I remember rightly, this latter was the regular *cayote* (pronounced ky-o-te) of the farther deserts. And if it was, he was not a pretty creature or respectable either, for I got well acquainted with his race afterward, and can speak with confidence. The cayote is a long, slim, sick and sorry-looking

TRUE WILLIAMS, *ROUGHING IT*, 1872, PAGE 51

skeleton, with a gray wolf-skin stretched over it, a tolerably bushy tail that forever sags down with a despairing expression of forsakenness and misery, a furtive and evil eye, and a long, sharp face, with slightly lifted lip and exposed teeth. He has a general slinking expression all over. The cayote is a living, breathing allegory of Want. He is *always* hungry. He is always poor, out of luck and friendless. The meanest creatures despise him, and even the fleas would desert him for a velocipede. He is so spiritless and cowardly that even while his exposed teeth are pretending a threat, the rest of his face is apologizing for it. And he is so homely!—so scrawny, and ribby, and coarse-haired, and pitiful. When he sees you he lifts his lip and lets a flash of his teeth out, and then turns a little out of the course he was pursuing, depresses his head a bit, and strikes a long, soft-footed trot through the sage-brush; glancing over his shoulder at you, from time to time till he is about out of easy pistol range, and then he stops and takes a deliberate survey of you; he will trot fifty yards and stop again—another fifty and stop again; and finally the gray of his gliding body blends with the gray of the sage-brush, and he disappears. All this is when you make no demonstration against him; but if you do, he develops a livelier interest in his journey, and instantly electrifies his heels and puts such a deal of real estate between himself and your weapon, that by the time you have raised the hammer you see that you need a minie rifle, and by the time you have got him in line you need a rifled cannon, and by the time you have "drawn a bead" on him you see well enough that nothing but an unusually long-winded streak of lightning could reach him where he is now. But if you start a swift-footed dog after him, you will enjoy it ever so much—especially if it is a dog that has a good opinion of himself, and has been brought up to think he knows something about speed. The cayote will go swinging gently off on that deceitful trot of his, and every little while he will smile a fraudful smile over his shoulder that will fill that dog entirely full of encouragement and worldly ambition, and make him lay his head still lower to the ground, and stretch his neck further to the front, and pant more fiercely, and stick his tail out straighter behind, and move his furious legs with a yet wilder frenzy, and leave a broader and broader, and higher and denser cloud of desert sand smoking behind, and marking his long wake across the level plain! And all this time the dog is only a short twenty feet behind the cayote, and to save the soul of him he cannot understand why it is that he cannot get perceptibly closer; and he begins to get aggravated, and it makes him madder and madder to see how gently the cayote glides along and never pants or sweats or ceases to smile; and he grows still more and more incensed to see how shamefully he has been taken in by an entire stranger, and what an ignoble swindle that long, calm, soft-footed trot is; and next he notices that he is getting fagged, and that the cayote actually has to slacken speed a little to keep from running away from him—and *then* that town-dog is mad in earnest, and he begins to strain and weep and swear, and paw the sand higher than ever, and reach for the cayote with concentrated and desperate energy. This "spurt" finds him six feet behind the gliding enemy, and two miles from his friends. And then, in the instant that a wild new hope is lighting up his face, the cayote turns and smiles blandly upon him once more, and with a something about it which seems to say: "Well, I shall have to tear myself away from you, bub—business is business, and it will not do for me to be fooling along this way all day"—and forthwith there is a rushing sound, and the sudden splitting of a long crack through the atmosphere, and behold that dog is solitary and alone in the midst of a vast solitude!

It makes his head swim. He stops, and looks all around; climbs the nearest sand-mound, and gazes into the distance; shakes his head reflectively, and then, without a word, he turns and jogs along back to his train, and takes up a humble position under the hindmost wagon, and feels unspeakably mean, and looks ashamed, and hangs his tail at half-mast for a week. And for as much as a year after that, whenever there is a great hue and cry after a cayote, that dog will merely glance in that direction without emotion, and apparently observe to himself, "I believe I do not wish any of the pie."

*If Mark Twain's scrawny allegory of want makes you think of the coyote (*Dogius ignoramus*) in Chuck Jones's popular Roadrunner cartoons, there's a good reason. Jones got his idea for Wile E. Coyote from the forlorn critter in* Roughing It. *Without Mark Twain, there never would have been a Wile E. Coyote or a Roadrunner!*

15.

A DOG OF A GRAVE AND
SERIOUS TURN OF MIND

———— •• • •••——

*Roughing It also describes a domestic dog that recklessly jumped
into California's strongly alkaline Mono Lake and emerged a rival
of the coyote in speed. That unusual body of water is ringed by tens
of millions of alkali flies with the disconcerting ability to travel
underwater in private air bubbles. The tiny insects live only a few
days as adults, but as the dog's experience shows, that's more than
long enough to cause trouble.*

———— •• • •••——

Mono Lake . . . is two hundred feet deep, and its
sluggish waters are so strong with alkali that if
you only dip the most hopelessly soiled garment
into them once or twice, and wring it out, it will be found as
clean as if it had been through the ablest of washerwomen's
hands. While we camped there our laundry work was easy. We

ROUGHING IT (1872), PAGE 266

tied the week's washing astern of our boat, and sailed a quarter
of a mile, and the job was complete, all to the wringing out. If
we threw the water on our heads and gave them a rub or so,
the white lather would pile up three inches high. This water is
not good for bruised places and abrasions of the skin. We had
a valuable dog. He had raw places on him. He had more raw
places on him than sound ones. He was the rawest dog I almost
ever saw. He jumped overboard one day to get away from the
flies. But it was bad judgment. In his condition, it would have
been just as comfortable to jump into the fire. The alkali water
nipped him in all the raw places simultaneously, and he struck
out for the shore with considerable interest. He yelped and
barked and howled as he went—and by the time he got to the
shore there was no bark to him—for he had barked the bark all

out of his inside, and the alkali water had cleaned the bark all off his outside, and he probably wished he had never embarked in any such enterprise. He ran round and round in a circle, and pawed the earth and clawed the air, and threw double somersaults, sometimes backward and sometimes forward, in the most extraordinary manner. He was not a demonstrative dog, as a general thing, but rather of a grave and serious turn of mind, and I never saw him take so much interest in anything before. He finally struck out over the mountains, at a gait which we estimated at about two hundred and fifty miles an hour, and he is going yet. This was about nine years ago. We look for what is left of him along here every day.

———————————— ✦ ————————————

On October 9, 1921, almost fifty years after Mark Twain wrote that passage, the Salt Lake Telegram *reported Californians were finally taking note of what he had said about the mineral powers of Mono Lake water. A company was formed to extract from the water salts for use in washing powder, shampoos, and other purposes.*

———————————— ✦ ————————————

16.

THE DOG THAT WARN'T
APP'NTED

———————◆———————

One of Roughing It*'s best-known anecdotes is Jim Blaine's "Story of the Old Ram," which fills up most of chapter 53. Every time the drunken old prospector tries to tell the story, he goes off on so many irrelevant tangents that he invariably falls asleep before reaching its end. Along the way, he talks about a missionary "et up by savages," pointing out that "prov'dence don't fire no blank ca'tridges" and that the missionary's being eaten was no accident. That leads him in still another direction—this one involving an alert dog. Unfortunately, before we learn more about the dog, Blaine starts off on yet another tangent. One wonders if Mark Twain got his idea for Blaine from the pilot William Brown, whom he had known on the Mississippi River. Like Blaine, Brown can't stick to one subject while telling a story (see chapter 2).*

———————◆———————

F. A. FRASER, *ROUGHING IT AND THE INNO-CENTS AT HOME*, CHATTO, 1906, PAGE 314

There ain't no such a thing as an accident. When my uncle Lem was leaning up agin a scaffolding once, sick, or drunk, or suthin, an Irishman with a hod full of bricks fell on him out of the third story and broke the old man's back in two places. People said it was an accident. Much accident there was about that. He didn't know what he was there for, but he was there for a good object. If he hadn't been there the Irishman would have been killed. Nobody can ever make me believe anything different from that. Uncle Lem's dog was there. Why didn't the Irishman fall on the dog? Becuz the dog would a seen him a coming and stood from under. That's the reason the dog warn't appinted. A dog can't be depended on to carry out a special providence. Mark my words it was a put-up thing. Accidents don't happen, boys. Uncle Lem's dog—I wish you could a seen that dog. He was a reglar shepherd—or ruther he was part bull and part shepherd—splendid animal; belonged to parson Hagar before Uncle Lem got him. Parson Hagar belonged to the Western Reserve Hagars . . .

17.

AN AWFUL, SOLID DOG

Jim Blaine isn't the only drunk in Roughing It *with a dog story. The dog in this next passage, however, is of a much more stolid (and solid) nature than Uncle Lem's dog. If a load of bricks were to fall on it, it wouldn't move a muscle to get out of the way.*

One drunken man necessarily reminds one of another. . . . Naturally, another gentleman present told about another drunken man. He said he reeled toward home late at night; made a mistake and entered the wrong gate; thought he saw a dog on the stoop; and it was—an iron one. He stopped and considered; wondered if it was a dangerous dog; ventured to say "Be (hic) begone!" No effect. Then he approached warily, and adopted conciliation; pursed up his lips and tried to whistle, but failed; still approached, saying,

COLLECTION OF THE EDITOR

"Poor dog!—doggy, doggy, doggy!—poor doggy-dog!" Got up on the stoop, still petting with fond names; till master of the advantages; then exclaimed, "Leave, you thief!"—planted a vindictive kick in his ribs, and went head-over-heels overboard, of course. A pause; a sigh or two of pain, and then a remark in a reflective voice:

"Awful solid dog. What could he ben eating? ('ic!) Rocks, p'raps. Such animals is dangerous. 'At's what I say—they're dangerous. If a man—('ic!)—if a man wants to feed a dog on rocks, let him feed him on rocks; 'at's all right; but let him keep him at home—not have him layin' round promiscuous, where ('ic!) where people's liable to stumble over him when they ain't noticin'!"

This passage reads like a rehearsal for the moment in Huckleberry Finn *in which Huck's drunken father, Pap, gives a tub of salt pork "a rattling kick" with "the boot that had a couple of his toes leaking out of the front end of it; so now he raised a howl that fairly made a body's hair raise . . ."*

Mark Twain seems to have found heavy metal objects such as anvils and cast-iron dogs funny, as they pop up throughout his writings. His autobiography, for example, discusses medical remedies in rural Missouri and recalls old women who gathered their own medicines in the woods, and "knew how to compound doses that would stir the vitals of a cast-iron dog."

18.

THE BULL PUP WITH
A GLASS EYE

In early 1894, while Mark Twain was between trips to Europe, a St. Louis Republic reporter interviewed him in New York. The disjointed remarks attributed to him in the published interview make one wonder if the reporter actually talked to him, or if he wrote his story after drinking too much Red-eye and reading Jim Blaine's "Story of the Old Ram" in Roughing It *(see chapter 16). The interview begins by quoting Mark Twain.*

"I had originally made up my mind to remain about five weeks, but my memory is so wretched that I find it difficult to remember how long I had intended to stay. That recalls the wonderful memory that old black cat of ours had. She did have the most remarkable memory of any cat almost I ever knew. Why, once she came into the kitchen and sat down on a hot stove lid, and do you know that ever after that, as long as we had her, she never sat down on a hot stove lid again? She wouldn't even sit down on a cold stove lid. At one time I thought it was her sagacity, but now I know it was her memory. She was like the bull pup that belongs to Miss Apple's old uncle, Ezra Pilkins. He was a wonderful old fellow. Had a bald head all his life from his babyhood. He never did have a single hair on his head, so old Marm Wilson said. Marm Wilson lived in the family, you know, for years and years, and I don't believe she would have left them if it hadn't been for the accident to young Jabel Endicott. That was the most peculiar accident I ever heard of. You see, Jabel was acquainted with Miss Appleby, and he used to visit her house a good deal and people said he was going to marry her. Well, her uncle's bull pup had one of his eyes put out when he was very young, and Jabel bought a glass eye and fitted it into the socket.

"It was not exactly a match to the other eye because the oculist that Jabel got it from only kept human glass eyes. Said he had never kept a stock of bull pup's glass eyes, anyhow. So Elihu Vedder—that was the name of the pup—used to wear the light blue glass eye, and he did have the strongest expression of most any dog I ever saw on the left side of his head— that was the side the glass eye was on. He was mightily proud of that glass eye, though. He used to kind of sidle up with his left side turned to strangers just so that they'd notice the eye and they always did notice it, too. Well, one day—"

"Excuse me, Mr. Clemens, but really about this European trip. If you—"

"Well, I was coming to that. As I said, one day, while Elihu Vedder was feeling so cocky about this glass eye of his and poking it under everybody's nose, so to speak, a strange bull dog came along. He walked up to Elihu in the friendliest kind of way and there wouldn't have been any trouble at all if Elihu hadn't tried to show that eye of his. He turned it suddenly on the other dog, and kind of lifted his nose in the air in a superior, supercilious sort of way. That made the other dog mad clean through and he made a jump for Elihu and grabbed him by the throat. Just then Jabel came along to call on Miss Appleby and when he saw her uncle's bull pup being choked by a strange dog he sailed in to separate them. In doing this he jabbed his finger into Elihu Vedder's glass eye and cut it most off. Of course he pulled his finger out again right away, but—"

"Mr. Clemens, I don't like to interrupt you, but if you will tell me just a little about your plans I would be greatly obliged."

A real Elihu Vedder (1836–1923) was an American painter probably best known at the time for his illustrations of The Rubáiyát of Omar Khayyám. *He and Mark Twain were slightly acquainted.*

19.

THE MOST PRECIOUS DOG
IN THE WORLD

———————•———————

Mark Twain's 1897 travel book, Following the Equator, *covers the round-the-world lecture tour that took him to Fiji, Australia, New Zealand, India, and South Africa. Its chapters on Australia naturally have much to say about kangaroos, but it was the dingo that won his heart. That was because he believed that wild dog species lacked what he most disliked about the canine species—their ability to bark. He first learned about the dingo during his trans-Pacific voyage, on which he met a young Englishman who bombarded him with scientific facts.*

———————•———————

He told me a great deal about worms, and the kangaroo, and other coleoptera, and said he knew the history and ways of all such pachydermata. He said the kangaroo had pockets, and carried its young in them when it couldn't get apples. And he said that the emu was as big as an ostrich, and looked like one, and had an amorphous appetite and would eat bricks. Also, that the dingo was not a dingo at all, but just a wild dog; and that the only difference between a dingo and a dodo was that neither of them barked; otherwise they were just the same.

———————

Although the young Englishman's dingo facts were not all strictly perpendicular, Mark Twain was sufficiently intrigued to investigate the animal further when he reached Australia.

———————

In that [Adelaide] garden I also saw the wild Australian dog— the dingo. He was a beautiful creature—shapely, graceful, a little wolfish in some of his aspects, but with a most friendly eye and sociable disposition. The dingo is not an importation; he was present in great force when the whites first came to the continent. It may be that he is the oldest dog in the universe; his origin, his descent, the place where his ancestors first appeared, are as unknown and as untraceable as are the camel's. He is the most precious dog in the world, for he does not bark. But in an evil hour he got to raiding the sheep-runs to appease his hunger, and that sealed his doom. He is hunted, now, just as if he were a wolf. He has been sentenced to extermination, and the sentence will be carried out.

Many Australian ranchers still regard dingoes as vermin, but, happily, the animals have not yet been exterminated. Dingoes can, incidentally, bark—but generally choose not to. In the matter of barking, perhaps a dingo is like Mark Twain was in the matter of lying. Mark Twain once explained how he differed from George Washington, who could not tell a lie. "As for me," he added, "I can, but I won't."

Mark Twain interrupted his visit to Australia with an extended tour of New Zealand, another British colony that interested him greatly. His private notebooks contain this remark about New Zealand.

Plenty dogs attend my lectures. They have had a fight only once, at Omoru. At Napier, sign up, "Dogs positively forbidden in the dress circle." Tacit permission to fill up the rest of the house.

"Dress circle" is a British term for what were usually the best seats in a theater, taking their name from the expectation that audience members in those seats were to dress formally. The theater in Napier evidently did not trust dogs to meet that standard.

20.

A REPTILIAN KIND OF DOG

Several years after writing A Dog's Tale *(see chapter 28) to raise public awareness of cruelties inflicted on animals in the name of science, Mark Twain wrote* A Horse's Tale *to help stir public sentiment against Spanish bullfighting. Soldier Boy, the story's central figure, is a scout horse on a western cavalry base. Like Rin Tin Tin of twentieth-century films and television, Shekels is the army base's mascot dog. Soldier Boy himself describes the dog in the conversation with another horse that follows below. While it is clear the terminology of the two horses is shaky, it is equally clear that Shekels is a remarkable dog. This tale, incidentally, is a rare example of a Mark Twain story in which animals talk to one another.*

"Who is Shekels?"

"The Seventh Cavalry dog. I mean, if he *is* a dog. His father was a coyote and his mother was a wild-cat. It doesn't really make a dog out of him, does it?"

"Not a real dog, I should think. Only a kind of a general dog, at most, I reckon. Though this is a matter of ichthyology, I suppose; and if it is, it is out of my depth, and so my opinion is not valuable, and I don't claim much consideration for it."

"It isn't ichthyology; it is dogmatics, which is still more difficult and tangled up. Dogmatics always are."

"Dogmatics is quite beyond me, quite; so I am not competing. But on general principles it is my opinion that a colt out of a coyote and a wild-cat is no square dog, but doubtful. That is my hand, and I stand pat."

"Well, it is as far as I can go myself, and be fair and conscientious. I have always regarded him as a doubtful dog, and so has Potter. Potter is the great Dane. Potter says he is no dog, and not even poultry—though I do not go quite so far as that."

"And I wouldn't, myself. Poultry is one of those things which no person can get to the bottom of, there is so much of it and such variety. It is just wings, and wings, and wings, till you are weary: turkeys, and geese, and bats, and butterflies, and angels, and grasshoppers, and flying-fish, and—well, there is really no end to the tribe; it gives me the heaves just to think of it. But this one hasn't any wings, has he?"

"Well, then, in my belief he is more likely to be dog than poultry. I have not heard of poultry that hadn't wings. Wings is the *sign* of poultry; it is what you tell poultry by. Look at the mosquito."

"What do you reckon he is, then? He must be something."

Soldier Boy watching over a young girl while wolves prowl around them. LUCIUS W. HITCH-COCK, *A HORSE'S TALE,* PAGE 92

"Why, he could be a reptile; anything that hasn't wings is a reptile."

"Who told you that?"

"Nobody told me, but I overheard it."

"Where did you overhear it?"

"Years ago. I was with the Philadelphia Institute expedition in the Bad Lands under Professor Cope, hunting mastodon bones, and I overheard him say, his own self, that any plantigrade circumflex vertebrate bacterium that hadn't wings and was uncertain was a reptile. Well, then, has this dog any wings? No. Is he a plantigrade circumflex vertebrate bacterium? Maybe so, maybe not; but without ever having seen him, and judging only by his illegal and spectacular parentage, I will bet the odds of a bale of hay to a bran mash that he looks it. Finally, is he uncertain? That is the point—is he uncertain? I will leave it to you if you have ever heard of a more uncertainer dog than what this one is?"

"No, I never have."

"Well, then, he's a reptile. That's settled."

"Why, look here, whatsyourname—"

"Last alias, Mongrel."

"A good one, too. I was going to say, you are better educated than you have been pretending to be. I like cultured society, and I shall cultivate your acquaintance. Now as to Shekels, whenever you want to know about any private thing that is going on at this post or in White Cloud's camp or Thunder-Bird's, he can tell you; and if you make friends with him he'll be glad to, for he is a born gossip, and picks up all the tittle-tattle. Being the whole Seventh Cavalry's reptile, he doesn't belong to anybody in particular, and hasn't any military duties; so he comes and goes as he pleases, and is popular with all the house cats and other authentic sources of private information. He understands all the languages, and talks them all, too. With an accent like gritting your teeth, it is true, and with a grammar that is no improvement on blasphemy—still, with practice you get at the meat of what he says, and it serves . . .

DANIEL BEARD, *CONNECTICUT YANKEE*, 1889, PAGE 54

PART III.

---·---

PUT-UPON POOCHES

Mark Twain was a harsh opponent of sentimentality in writing, but his resolve to shun that fault himself sometimes failed him when he wrote about mistreated animals like those in the following selections. More than a little sentimentality is evident in "A Judgment" and "A Dog's Tale" in this section. The latter story—which was published as a book—Mark Twain wrote in support of his daughter Jean's animal-rights causes.

In sharp contrast, some of these stories will demonstrate that he was anything but sentimental about animals early in his writing career. We know he was often striving for humor with satire, but occasionally a bit of a mean streak seems to show through his words.

21.

RULES TO SAVE THE CANINES

———— • ————

In 1866, Mark Twain was in San Francisco at a time when the city government raised a storm by having stray dogs shot (see chapter 3). In the burlesque article below, he offered some unusual advice for saving dogs from being shot. As harsh as that advice was, it must have caught the public fancy, as this article was reprinted in at least two dozen newspapers from coast to coast. Some dog lovers, however, may wish to skip this selection.

———— • ————

**MARK TWAIN ON THE DOG QUESTION
RULES TO SAVE THE CANINES.**

The philosopher and Independent Missionary puts forth the following rules, which will render a dog insensible to bullet wounds:

1. Take your dog (if he be a black dog, with spots on him) and soak him over night in a tank of turpentine, and then ignite him in the morning. After this, bullets cannot distress him.

2. If he be a thin-skinned dog of the species called Poodle, remove his internal arrangements carefully and fill him up with sawdust, sawdust is impervious to bullets.

3. If he be a valuable speckled dog, take off his hide and line it with sheet iron. Russia iron is best, and is slicker and more showy than the common kind. Dogs prepared in this way do not mind bullets.

4. The presence of the dog is often betrayed to the Policeman by his bark. Remove the bark from his system and your dog is safe. This may be done by mixing a spoonful of the soother called strychnine in his rations. It will be next to impossible to ever get that dog to bark any more.

5. When you see a Policeman coming after your dog, make the animal go off and get out of the way. It is easily accomplished. Let the dog eat a moderate quantity of nitro-glycerine— from four to sixteen pounds, according to his size—and bounce him on the ground a couple of times. This will make him go off.

6. But the surest and safest course to pursue, is always to keep your dog around where riots and other aggravated disturbances of the peace are going on.

22.

THE STORY OF THE GOOD LITTLE BOY WHO DID NOT PROSPER

———— •——•——•————

Late in his writing career, Mark Twain wrote what would become one of his most famous maxims: "If you pick up a starving dog and make him prosperous, he will not bite you. This is the principal difference between a dog and a man." He evidently had a very different view on that subject when he wrote this cautionary tale in 1870.

———— •——•——•————

Once there was a good little boy by the name of Jacob Blivens. He always obeyed his parents, no matter how absurd and unreasonable their demands were; and he always learned his book, and never was late at Sabbath school. He would not play hookey, even when his sober judgment told him it was the most profitable thing he could do. None of the other boys could ever make that boy out, he acted so strangely. He wouldn't lie, no matter how convenient it was. He just said it was wrong to lie, and that was sufficient for him. And he was so honest that he was simply ridiculous. The curious ways that that Jacob had surpassed everything. He wouldn't play marbles on Sunday, he wouldn't rob birds' nests, he wouldn't give hot pennies to organ-grinders' monkeys; he didn't seem to take any interest in any kind of rational amusement. So the other boys used to try to reason it out and come to an understanding of him, but they couldn't arrive at any satisfactory conclusion; as I said before, they could only figure out a sort of vague idea that he was "afflicted,"

F. M. SENIOR, *PUDD'NHEAD WILSON*, 1894, PAGE 214

and so they took him under their protection, and never allowed any harm to come to him.

This good little boy read all the Sunday-school books; they were his greatest delight. This was the whole secret of it. He believed in the good little boys they put in the Sunday-school books; he had every confidence in them. He longed to come across one of them alive, once; but he never did. They all died before his time, maybe. Whenever he read about a particularly good one, he turned over quickly to the end to see what became of him, because he wanted to travel thousands of miles and gaze on him; but it wasn't any use; that good little boy always died in the last chapter, and there was a picture of the funeral, with all his relations and the Sunday-school children standing around the grave in pantaloons that were too short, and bonnets that were too large, and everybody crying into handkerchiefs that had as much as a yard and a half of stuff in them. He was always headed off in this way. He never could see one of those good little boys, on account of his always dying in the last chapter.

Jacob had a noble ambition to be put in a Sunday-school book. He wanted to be put in, with pictures representing him gloriously declining to lie to his mother, and she weeping for joy about it; and pictures representing him standing on the doorstep giving a penny to a poor beggar-woman with six children, and telling her to spend it freely, but not to be extravagant, because extravagance is a sin; and pictures of him magnanimously refusing to tell on the bad boy who always lay in wait for him around the corner, as he came from school, and welted him over the head with a lath, and then chased him home, saying "Hi! hi!" as he proceeded. That was the ambition of young Jacob. He wished to be put in a Sunday-school book. It made him feel a little uncomfortable sometimes when he reflected that the good little boys always died. He loved to

TRUE WILLIAMS, *SKETCHES NEW & OLD*, 1875, PAGE 58

live, you know, and this was the most unpleasant feature about being a Sunday-school-book boy. He knew it was not healthy to be good. He knew it was more fatal than consumption to be so supernaturally good as the boys in the books were; he knew that none of them had ever been able to stand it long, and it pained him to think that if they put him in a book he wouldn't ever see it, or even if they did get the book out before he died, it wouldn't be popular without any picture of his funeral in the back part of it. It couldn't be much of a Sunday-school book that couldn't tell about the advice he gave to the community when he was dying. So, at last, of course he had to make up his mind to do the best he could under the circumstances—to live right, and hang on as long as he could, and have his dying speech all ready when his time came.

But somehow, nothing ever went right with this good little boy; nothing ever turned out with him the way it turned out with the good little boys in the books. They always had a good time, and the bad boys had the broken legs; but in his case there was a screw loose somewhere, and it all happened, just the other way. When he found Jim Blake stealing apples and went under the tree to read to him about the bad little boy who fell out of a neighbor's apple tree, and broke his arm, Jim fell out of the tree too, but he fell on him, and broke his arm, and Jim wasn't hurt at all. Jacob couldn't understand that. There wasn't anything in the books like it.

And once, when some bad boys pushed a blind man over in the mud, and Jacob ran to help him up and receive his blessing, the blind man did not give him any blessing at all, but whacked him over the head with his stick and said he would like to catch him shoving him again and then pretending to help him up. This was not in accordance with any of the books. Jacob looked them all over to see.

One thing that Jacob wanted to do was to find a lame dog that hadn't any place to stay, and was hungry and persecuted, and bring him home and pet him and have that dog's imperishable gratitude. And at last he found one, and was happy; and he brought him home and fed him, but when he was going to pet him the dog flew at him and tore all the clothes off him except those that were in front, and made a spectacle of him that was astonishing. He examined authorities, but he could not understand the matter. It was of the same breed of dogs that was in the books, but it acted very differently. Whatever this boy did, he got into trouble. The very things the boys in the books got rewarded for turned out to be about the most unprofitable things he could invest in.

Once when he was on his way to Sunday school he saw some bad boys starting off pleasuring in a sail-boat. He was filled with consternation, because he knew from his reading that boys who went sailing on Sunday invariably got drowned. So he ran out on a raft to warn them, but a log turned with him and slid him into the river. A man got him out pretty soon, and the doctor pumped the water out of him and gave him a fresh start with his bellows, but he caught cold and lay sick abed nine weeks. But the most unaccountable thing about it was that the bad boys in the boat had a good time all day, and then reached home alive and well in the most surprising manner. Jacob Blivens said there was nothing like these things in the books. He was perfectly dumbfounded.

When he got well he was a little discouraged, but he resolved to keep on trying, anyhow. He knew that so far his experiences wouldn't do to go in a book, but he hadn't yet reached the allotted term of life for good little boys, and he hoped to be able to make a record yet, if he could hold on till his time was fully up. If everything else failed, he had his dying speech to fall back on.

He examined his authorities, and found that it was now time for him to go to sea as a cabin boy. He called on a ship captain and made his application, and when the captain asked for his recommendations he proudly drew out a tract and pointed to the words: "To Jacob Blivens, from his affectionate teacher." But the captain was a coarse, vulgar man, and he said, "Oh, that be blowed! *that* wasn't any proof that he knew how to wash dishes or handle a slush-bucket, and he guessed he didn't want him." This was altogether the most extraordinary thing that ever had happened to Jacob in all his life. A compliment from a teacher, on a tract, had never failed to move the tenderest of emotions of ship captains and open the way to all offices of honor and profit in their gift—it never had in any book that ever he had read. He could hardly believe his senses.

This boy always had a hard time of it. Nothing ever came out according to the authorities with him. At last, one day, when he was around hunting up bad little boys to admonish, he found a lot of them in the old iron foundry fixing up a little joke on fourteen or fifteen dogs, which they had tied together in long procession and were going to ornament with empty nitro-glycerine cans made fast to their tails. Jacob's heart was touched. He sat down on one of those cans—for he never

A. B. FROST, *CARLO*, DOUBLEDAY, 1913, PAGE 27

minded grease when duty was before him—and he took hold
of the foremost dog by the collar, and turned his reproving eye
upon wicked Tom Jones. But just at that moment Alderman
McWelter, full of wrath, stepped in. All the bad boys ran away;
but Jacob Blivens rose in conscious innocence and began one of
those stately little Sunday-school book speeches which always
commence with "Oh, Sir!" in dead opposition to the fact that
no boy, good or bad, ever starts a remark with "Oh, Sir!" But
the Alderman never waited to hear the rest. He took Jacob
Blivens by the ear and turned him around, and hit him a whack
in the rear with the flat of his hand; and in an instant that good
little boy shot out through the roof and soared away toward
the sun, with the fragments of those fifteen dogs stringing

after him like the tail of a kite. And there wasn't a sign of that Alderman or that old iron foundry left on the face of the earth; and as for young Jacob Blivens, he never got a chance to make his last dying speech after all his trouble fixing it up, unless he made it to the birds; because, although the bulk of him came down all right in a tree-top in an adjoining county, the rest of him was apportioned around among four townships, and so they had to hold five inquests on him to find out whether he was dead or not, and how it occurred. You never saw a boy scattered so.

Thus perished the good little boy who did the best he could, but didn't come out according to the books. Every boy who ever did as he did prospered, except him. His case is truly remarkable. It will probably never be accounted for.

23.

A DOG MERETRICIOUS IN HIS MOVEMENTS

———••◆•——

Soon after arriving in Nevada in 1861, Mark Twain helped form a prospecting party with three other men and a dog and headed north to the Humboldt district's promising mining fields. Among his companions was a much older man—called "Ballou" in Roughing It—*who was notorious for fracturing English. For example, he attributed the exhaustion of the party's horses to their "being 'bituminous from long deprivation.' . . . If a word was long and grand and resonant, that was sufficient to win the old man's love, and he would drop that word into the most out-of-the-way place in a sentence or a subject, and be as pleased with it as if it were perfectly luminous with meaning."*

———••◆•——

ROUGHING IT, 1872, PAGE 181

We four always spread our common stock of blankets together on the frozen ground, and slept side by side; and finding that our foolish, long-legged hound pup had a deal of animal heat in him, Oliphant got to admitting him to the bed, between himself and Mr. Ballou, hugging the dog's warm back to his breast and finding great comfort in it. But in the night the pup would get stretchy and brace his feet against the old man's back and shove, grunting complacently the while; and now and then, being warm and snug, grateful and happy, he would paw the old man's back simply in excess of comfort; and at yet other times he would dream of the chase and in his sleep tug at the old man's back hair and bark in his ear. The old gentleman complained mildly about these familiarities, at last, and when he got through with his statement he said that such a dog as that was not a proper animal to admit to bed with tired men, because he was "so meretricious in his movements and so organic in his emotions." We turned the dog out.

24.

OUTFOXING THE FOX HUNTERS

———————◆———————

In 1895, Mark Twain encountered an acquaintance in Australia who brought up the name of an English earl whom both had known. That remark reminded Mark Twain of an English foxhunt at which he had met the earl many years earlier. This description of that hunt—and its illustration—show that his sympathies clearly lay with that close relative of the dog, the fox, not with the hunters.

In English foxhunts, horseback riders follow packs of hounds that chase foxes across the countryside. The object of hunts is not always to kill the foxes, but that is often the unhappy result when the dogs reach the foxes first. Fortunately, times have changed. Hunting foxes with dogs has been banned throughout Great Britain since 2005.

———————◆———————

I t was a quarter of a century ago—1873 or '74. I had an American friend in London named F., who was fond of hunting, and his friends the Blanks invited him and me to come out to a hunt and be their guests at their country place. In the morning the mounts were provided, but when I saw the horses I changed my mind and asked permission to walk. I had never seen an English hunt before, and it seemed to me that I could hunt a fox safer on the ground. I had always been diffident about horses, anyway, even those of the common altitudes, and I did not feel competent to hunt on a horse that went on stilts. So then Mrs. Blank came to my help and said I could go with her in the dog-cart and we would drive to a place she knew of, and there we should have a good glimpse of the hunt as it went by.

"When we got to that place I got out and went and leaned my elbows on a low stone wall which enclosed a turfy and beautiful great field with heavy wood on all its sides except ours. Mrs. Blank sat in the dog-cart fifty yards away, which was as near as she could get with the vehicle. I was full of interest, for I had never seen a fox-hunt. I waited, dreaming and imagining, in the deep stillness and impressive tranquillity which reigned in that retired spot. Presently, from away off in the forest on the left, a mellow bugle-note came floating; then all of a sudden a multitude of dogs burst out of that forest and went tearing by and disappeared in the forest on the right; there was a pause, and then a cloud of horsemen in black caps and crimson coats plunged out of the left-hand forest and went flaming across the field like a prairie-fire, a stirring sight to see. There was one man ahead of the rest, and he came spurring straight at me. He was fiercely excited. It was fine to see him ride; he was a master horseman. He came like a storm till he was within seven feet of me, where I was leaning on the wall,

DANIEL BEARD, *FOLLOWING THE EQUATOR*, 1897, PAGE 198

then he stood his horse straight up in the air on his hind toe-nails, and shouted like a demon:

"Which, way'd the fox go?"

I didn't much like the tone, but I did not let on; for he was excited, you know. But I was calm; so I said softly, and without acrimony: "Which fox?"

It seemed to anger him. I don't know why; and he thundered out: "*Which* fox? Why, *the* fox! Which way did the *fox* go?"

I said, with great gentleness—even argumentatively: "If you could be a little more definite—a little less vague—because I am a stranger, and there are many foxes, as you will know even better than I, and unless I know which one it is that you desire to identify, and—"

"You're certainly the damnedest idiot that has escaped in a thousand years!" and he snatched his great horse around as easily as I would snatch a cat, and was away like a hurricane. A very excitable man.

I went back to Mrs. Blank, and she was excited, too—oh, all alive. She said: "He *spoke* to you!—*didn't* he?"

"Yes, it is what happened."

"I *knew* it! I couldn't hear what he said, but I knew he spoke to you! Do you know who it was? It was Lord C.,—and he is Master of the Buckhounds! Tell me—what do you think of him?"

"Him? Well, for sizing-up a stranger, he's got the most sudden and accurate judgment of any man I ever saw."

It pleased her. I thought it would.

25.

CAMELOT–AN UNCONGENIAL SPOT FOR DOGS?

———••—•—••———

In Mark Twain's 1889 novel, A Connecticut Yankee in King Arthur's Court, *Hank Morgan is mysteriously transported to sixth-century England, where almost immediately he encounters "troops of dogs." A knight then captures him and takes him to King Arthur's castle in Camelot. There, Hank describes a raucous assemblage of people and a larger and even more raucous assemblage of ill-treated dogs. He soon learns there's simply not a less congenial spot for canine happily-ever-aftering than there in Camelot.*

———••—•—••———

Mainly they were drinking—from entire ox horns; but a few were still munching bread or gnawing beef bones. There was about an average of two dogs to one man; and these sat in expectant attitudes till a spent bone was flung to them, and then they went for it by brigades

DANIEL BEARD, *CONNECTICUT YANKEE*, 1889, PAGE 46

and divisions, with a rush, and there ensued a fight which filled the prospect with a tumultuous chaos of plunging heads and bodies and flashing tails, and the storm of howlings and barkings deafened all speech for the time; but that was no matter, for the dog-fight was always a bigger interest anyway; the men rose, sometimes, to observe it the better and bet on it, and the ladies and the musicians stretched themselves out over their balusters with the same object; and all broke into delighted ejaculations from time to time. In the end, the winning dog stretched himself out comfortably with his bone between his paws, and proceeded to growl over it, and gnaw it, and grease the floor with it, just as fifty others were already doing; and

DANIEL BEARD, *CONNECTICUT YANKEE*, 1889, PAGE 54

the rest of the court resumed their previous industries and entertainments.

As a rule, the speech and behavior of these people were gracious and courtly; and I noticed that they were good and serious listeners when anybody was telling anything—I mean in a dog-fightless interval. And plainly, too, they were a child-like and innocent lot; telling lies of the stateliest pattern with a most gentle and winning naivety, and ready and willing to listen to anybody else's lie, and believe it, too. It was hard to associate them with anything cruel or dreadful; and yet they dealt in tales of blood and suffering with a guileless relish that made me almost forget to shudder. . . .

In the next chapter the old wizard Merlin narrates a tedious and often-told tale that puts everyone—including the dogs—to sleep.

Sir Dinadan the Humorist was the first to awake, and he soon roused the rest with a practical joke of a sufficiently poor quality. He tied some metal mugs to a dog's tail and turned him loose, and he tore around and around the place in a frenzy of fright, with all the other dogs bellowing after him and battering and crashing against everything that came in their way and making altogether a chaos of confusion and a most deafening din and turmoil; at which every man and woman of the multitude laughed till the tears flowed, and some fell out of their chairs and wallowed on the floor in ecstasy. It was just like so many children. Sir Dinadan was so proud of his exploit that he could not keep from telling over and over again, to weariness, how the immortal idea happened to occur to him; and as is the way with humorists of his breed, he was still laughing at it after everybody else had got through . . .

Mark Twain often expressed contempt for people who played mean tricks on animals. The knights of sixth-century England weren't the only animal abusers he targeted. In chapter 21 of Adventures of Huckleberry Finn *(1885), for example, Huck observes the cruel behavior of loafers in a decaying river town that is even less congenial to dogs than Camelot.*

━━━━━•◆•━━━━━

All the streets and lanes was just mud, they warn't nothing else but mud—mud as black as tar, and nigh about a foot deep in some places; and two or three inches deep in all the places. The hogs loafed and grunted around, everywheres. You'd see a muddy sow and a litter of pigs come lazying along the street and whollop herself right down in the way, where folks had to walk around her, and she'd stretch out, and shut her eyes, and wave her ears, whilst the pigs was milking her, and look as happy as if she was on salary. And pretty soon you'd hear a loafer sing out, "Hi! *so* boy! sick him, Tige!" and away the sow would go, squealing most horrible, with a dog or two swinging to each ear, and three or four dozen more a-coming; and then you would see all the loafers get up and watch the thing out of sight, and laugh at the fun and look grateful for the noise. Then they'd settle back again till there was a dog-fight. There couldn't anything wake them up all over, and make them happy all over, like a dog-fight—unless it might be putting turpentine on a stray dog and setting fire to him, or tying a tin to his tail and see him run himself to death.

26.

HOW "PUDD'NHEAD" WILSON GOT HIS NAME

———————•———————

Pudd'nhead Wilson, *published in 1894, is one of Mark Twain's most widely read and admired novels, but how many people realize its unusual title has something to do with a dog? The title comes from the unfortunate nickname bestowed upon the young attorney David Wilson the day he arrives in a Missouri village and is heard to utter a strange remark about a yelping dog. It seems a little unfair for Wilson to get tagged a "pudd'nhead" for doing that, instead of Mark Twain, as his remark is exactly the sort of thing Mark Twain might have said himself.*

———————•———————

In that same month of February, Dawson's Landing gained a new citizen. This was Mr. David Wilson, a young fellow of Scotch parentage. He had wandered to this remote region from his birthplace in the interior of the State of New

York, to seek his fortune. He was twenty-five years old, college-bred, and had finished a post-college course in an Eastern law school a couple of years before.

He was a homely, freckled, sandy-haired young fellow, with an intelligent blue eye that had frankness and comradeship in it and a covert twinkle of a pleasant sort. But for an unfortunate remark of his, he would no doubt have entered at once upon a successful career at Dawson's Landing. But he made his fatal remark the first day he spent in the village, and it "gaged" him. He had just made the acquaintance of a group of citizens when an invisible dog began to yelp and snarl and howl and make himself very comprehensively disagreeable, whereupon young Wilson said, much as one who is thinking aloud—"I wished I owned half of that dog."

"Why?" somebody asked.

"Because I would kill my half."

The group searched his face with curiosity, with anxiety even, but found no light there, no

F. M. SENIOR, *PUDD'NHEAD WILSON*, 1894, PAGE 24

expression that they could read. They fell away from him as from something uncanny, and went into privacy to discuss him. One said: "'Pears to be a fool."

"'Pears?" said another. "*Is*, I reckon you better say."

"Said he wished he owned *half* of the dog, the idiot," said a third. "What did he reckon would become of the other half if he killed his half? Do you reckon he thought it would live?"

"Why, he must have thought it, unless he *is* the downrightest fool in the world; because if he hadn't thought it, he would have wanted to own the whole dog, knowing that if he killed his half and the other half died, he would be responsible for that half just the same as if he had killed that half instead of his own. Don't it look that way to you, gents?"

"Yes, it does. If he owned one half of the general dog, it would be so; if he owned one end of the dog and another

F. M. SENIOR, *PUDD'NHEAD WILSON*, 1894, PAGE 24

person owned the other end, it would be so, just the same; particularly in the first case, because if you kill one half of a general dog, there ain't any man that can tell whose half it was, but if he owned one end of the dog, maybe he could kill his end of it and—"

"No, he couldn't, either: he couldn't and not be responsible if the other end died, which it would. In my opinion the man ain't in his right mind."

"In my opinion he hain't *got* any mind."

No. 3 said: "Well, he's a lummox, anyway."

"That's what he is," said No. 4, "he's a labrick—just a Simon-pure labrick, if ever there was one."

"Yes, sir, he's a dam fool, that's the way I put him up," said No. 5. "Anybody can think different that wants to, but those are my sentiments."

"I'm with you, gentlemen," said No. 6. "Perfect jackass— yes, and it ain't going too far to say he is a pudd'nhead. If he ain't a pudd'nhead, I ain't no judge, that's all."

Mr. Wilson stood elected. The incident was told all over the town, and gravely discussed by everybody. Within a week he had lost his first name; Pudd'nhead took its place. In time he came to be liked, and well liked too; but by that time the nickname had got well stuck on, and it stayed. That first day's verdict made him a fool, and he was not able to get it set aside, or even modified. The nickname soon ceased to carry any harsh or unfriendly feeling with it, but it held its place, and was to continue to hold its place for twenty long years.

27.

A JUDGMENT

This passage is from "The Enchanted Sea-Wilderness," one of many unfinished stories Mark Twain began late in his life. What happens to the heroic dog in Melvillian-flavored tragedy seems to confirm the cynical view of human gratitude Pudd'nhead Wilson expresses in his maxim about a starving dog (see chapter 22).

Scattered about the world's oceans at enormous distances apart are spots and patches where no compass has any value. When the compass enters one of these bewitched domains it goes insane and whirls this way and that and settles nowhere, and is scared and distressed, and cannot be comforted. The sailor must steer by sun, moon and stars when they show, and by guess when they don't, till he gets past that enchanted region. The worst of these spots and the largest one is in the midst of the vast ocean solitudes that lie between the

COURTESY LIBRARY OF CONGRESS

Cape of Good Hope and the south pole. It is five hundred miles in diameter, and is circular in shape; four-fifths of this diameter is lashed and tossed and torn by eternal storms, is smothered in clouds and fog, and swept by fierce concentric currents; but in the centre there is a circular area a hundred miles across, in whose outer part the storms and the currents die down; and in the centre of this centre there is still a final circular area about fifty miles across where there are but the faintest suggestions of currents, no winds, no whisper of wandering zephyr, even, but everywhere the silence and peace and solemnity of a calm which is eternal.

There is a bronzed and gray sailor on board this ship who has had experience of that strange place, and the other night after midnight I went forward to the forecastle and got him to tell me about it. The hint came from the purser, who said it was a curious and interesting story. I kept it in my memory as well as I could, and wrote it down next day—in my own language, for I could not remember his, of course. He said that the outer great circle where the currents are—as already described by me—is known among sailors as the Devil's Race-Track, and that they call the central calm Everlasting Sunday. Here is his account.

THE ENCHANTED SEA-WILDERNESS.

We got into that place by a judgment—judgment on the captain of the ship. It was this way. We were becalmed, away down south, dead summer time, middle of December, 1853. The vessel was a brig, and a fairly good sailor; name, *Mabel Thorpe;* loaded with provisions and blasting powder for the new gold mines in Australia; Elliot Cable, master, a rough man and hard-hearted, but he *was* master, and that is the truth. When he laid down the law there wasn't pluck enough in the whole ship to take objections to it.

Now to go back a little. About two months before, when we were lying at the dock the day we sailed, a lovely big beautiful dog came aboard and went racing around with his nose down hunting for somebody that had been there—his owner, I reckon—and the crew caught him and shut him up below, and we sailed in an hour. He was a darling, that dog. He was full of play, and fun, and affection and good nature, the dearest and sweetest disposition that ever was. Inside of two days he was the pet of the whole crew. We bedded him like the aristocracy, and there wasn't a man but would divide his dinner with him, and he was ever so loving and grateful. And smart, too; smart and willing. He elected of his own notion to stand watch and watch with us. He was in the larboard watch, and he would turn out at eight bells without anybody having to tell him it was "Yo-ho, the larboard watch!" And he would tug at the ropes and help make sail or take it in, and seemed to know all about it, just like any old veteran. The crew were proud of him—well, of course they would be.

And so, as I was saying, we got becalmed when we were out about two months. It was warm that night, and still and drowsy and lazy; and the sails hung idle, and the deck-watch and the lookout and everybody else was sound asleep, including the dog, for it was his trick below and he had turned in at midnight. Well, along about an hour after midnight there was a tremendous scratching and barking at the captain's door, and he jumped out of his bunk, and that dog was just wild with excitement, and rushed off, and just as good as told the captain to come along and come quick. You see, the ship was afire down in the hold, and he had discovered it. Down the captain plunged, and the dog rushed off waking up the others.

Dear, dear, it was the closest fit! The fire was crowding a pile of the powder-kegs close, and in another minute or two it would have had them and we should have been blown into the sky. The captain snatched the pile of kegs out of reach in half a second, and we were safe; because the bulk of the powder was away up forward. And by this time we all came tearing down—white?—oh, white as ghosts when we saw what a close shave we had had. Well, then we started in and began to hug the dog. And wasn't he a proud dog?—and happy?—why, if he had had speech he couldn't have expressed it any better. The captain snarled at us and said:

"You may well hug him, you worthless hounds! he saved my life, not you, you lazy rips. I've never cared for dogs before, but next time I hear people talking against them I'll put in a word for this one, anyway."

Overboard went that little batch of powder kegs, and then we flew around getting food and water and compass and sextant and chart and things for the boat; and the dog helped, just like anybody else. He did a grown man's work carrying things to the boat, and then went dancing around superintending whilst we launched her. Bright?—oh, you can't think how bright he was, and intelligent.

When everybody was in the boat but the captain, and the flames were soaring up and lighting the whole ocean, he tied the dog to the foot of the mainmast and then got in himself and took the tiller and said—"All ready. Give way!"

We were all struck dumb, for a second, then all shouted at once, "Oh, *captain!*—going to leave the dog?"

He roared out in a fury—"Didn't you hear the order? Give way!"

Well, the tears began to run down our faces; and we said, Why, he saved our *lives*—we *can't* leave him. Please, captain! please let him come.

"What, in this little tub of a boat? You don't know what you are talking about. He'd be more in the way than a family of children; and he can eat as much as a family of children, too. Now, men, you know *me*"—and he pulled an old pepper-box revolver and pointed it—"give *way!*"

Well, it was pitiful, the way that poor dog acted. At first he was dancing and capering and barking, happy and proud and gay; but when he saw us going away he stopped and stood still, gazing; it seemed as if he was trying to believe it, and couldn't. And dear, dear, how noble and handsome he was, in that red glare. He was a huge big St. Bernard, with that gentle good face and that soft loving eye that they've got.

Well, pretty soon when he saw that he *was* left, he seemed to go kind of crazy; and he rose on his hind legs in the strong light, and strained and lunged and tugged at his rope, and begged and moaned and yelped—why it was as plain as if he was *saying* Oh, don't leave me, *please* don't leave me, I haven't done any harm. And then presently the fire swept down on him and swallowed him up, and he sent up two or three awful shrieks, and it was all over. And the men sat there crying like children.

And deep down in our hearts we believed a judgment would come on the captain for this. And it did; as you will see.

II

We were in the Indian ocean when we lost the ship—about five hundred miles south of Port Natal, and about the same distance east by south from Cape Town, South Africa. The captain set his course by the stars and struck north, because he believed we were a little south of the track of ships bound for either Natal or Australia. A smart breeze sprung up and we went along at a good rate. In about four hours day broke, and the first thing that showed up on the westward sea-line was the hazy top-hamper of a ship! She was eastward-bound, and making straight across our course. We raised a cheer, and altered our course to go and meet her. And there wasn't as much heart in the cheer as you might expect, for the thing we were thinking about was, that our poor dog had been done to death for no use; if he had been allowed to come with us he wouldn't have cost us any inconvenience, and no food that we couldn't spare.

The captain had an idea that he was born lucky, and he said something to the mate about it now; he said running across this ship here was pure luck—nobody else could have had such luck. Well, it certainly did look so; but at the same time we said to ourselves, how about this ship's luck that's coming? Our idea was that our captain would bring bad luck to her, and trouble to himself and us, too, on account of the way he treated the dog that saved our lives. And that is what happened, as I have said before.

———————— • • ————————

The story continues with the men boarding the other ship. That vessel turns out to be the Mabel Thorpe's *sister ship, the* Adelaide, *whose captain and several crew members have died from a mysterious illness. The* Mabel Thorpe's *captain peremptorily takes command and sets sail for Australia. However, the* Adelaide *never reaches that destination or any other. Instead, it becomes permanently becalmed in the ghostly region of the Everlasting Sunday, which is littered with other ships filled with decaying corpses.*

———————— • • ————————

28.

A DOG'S TALE

───────◆───────

The most sentimental work Mark Twain ever wrote is almost certainly A Dog's Tale, *which he published in a magazine in 1903 and as a small book the following year. A contemporary reviewer said of the story that "few can read it and not be moved to tears. It is one of those rare books which appeal to grown-ups and children." It is also, incidentally, one of Mark Twain's few stories narrated by an animal. Aileen Mavourneen, the simple, trusting canine narrator, tells a story of human ingratitude that does, indeed, reduce many readers to tears. The entire book follows below.*

───────◆───────

CHAPTER 1

My father was a St. Bernard, my mother was a collie, but I am a Presbyterian. This is what my mother told me, I do not know these nice distinctions myself. To me they are only fine large words meaning

nothing. My mother had a fondness for such; she liked to say them, and see other dogs look surprised and envious, as wondering how she got so much education. But, indeed, it was not real education; it was only show: she got the words by listening in the dining-room and drawing-room when there was company, and by going with the children to Sunday-school and listening there; and whenever she heard a large word she said it over to herself many times, and so was able to keep it until there was a dogmatic gathering in the neighborhood, then she would get it off, and surprise and distress them all, from pocket-pup to mastiff, which rewarded her for all her trouble. If there was a stranger he was nearly sure to be suspicious, and when he got his breath again he would ask her what it meant. And she always told him. He was never expecting this, but thought he would catch her; so when she told him, he was the one that looked ashamed, whereas he had thought it was going to be she. The others were always waiting for this, and glad of it and proud of her, for they knew what was going to happen, because they had had experience. When she told the meaning of a big word they were all so taken up with admiration that it never occurred to any dog to doubt if it was the right one; and that was natural, because, for one thing, she answered up so promptly that it seemed like a dictionary speaking, and for another thing, where could they find out whether it was right or not? for she was the only cultivated dog there was. By and by, when I was older, she brought home the word Unintellectual, one time, and worked it pretty hard all the week at different gatherings, making much unhappiness and despondency; and it was at this time that I noticed that during that week she was asked for the meaning at eight different assemblages, and flashed out a fresh definition every time, which showed me that she had more presence of mind than culture, though I said nothing, of course. She had one word which she always kept on hand, and ready, like a life-preserver, a kind of emergency word to strap on when she was likely to get washed overboard in a sudden way—that was the word Synonymous. When she happened to fetch out a long word which had had its day weeks before and its prepared meanings gone to her dump-pile, if there was a stranger there of course it knocked him groggy for a couple of minutes, then he would come to, and by that time she would be away down the wind on another tack, and not expecting anything; so when he'd hail and ask her to cash in, I (the only dog on the inside of her game) could see her canvas flicker a moment—but only just a moment—then it would belly out taut and full, and she would say, as calm as a summer's day, "It's synonymous with supererogation," or some godless long reptile of a word like that, and go placidly about and skim away on the next tack, perfectly comfortable, you know, and leave that stranger looking profane and embarrassed, and the initiated slatting the floor with their tails in unison and their faces transfigured with a holy joy.

And it was the same with phrases. She would drag home a whole phrase, if it had a grand sound, and play it six nights and two matinees, and explain it a new way every time—which she had to, for all she cared for was the phrase; she wasn't interested in what it meant, and knew those dogs hadn't wit enough to catch her, anyway. Yes, she was a daisy! She got so she wasn't afraid of anything, she had such confidence in the ignorance of those creatures. She even brought anecdotes that she had heard the family and the dinner-guests laugh and shout over; and as a rule she got the nub of one chestnut hitched onto another chestnut, where, of course, it didn't fit and hadn't any point; and when she delivered the nub she fell over and rolled on the floor and laughed and barked in the most insane way, while I could see that she was wondering to herself why it didn't seem as funny as it did when she first heard it. But no harm was done; the others rolled and barked too, privately ashamed of themselves for not seeing the point, and never suspecting that the fault was not with them and there wasn't any to see.

You can see by these things that she was of a rather vain and frivolous character; still, she had virtues, and enough to make up, I think. She had a kind heart and gentle ways, and never harbored resentments for injuries done her, but put them easily out of her mind and forgot them; and she taught her children her kindly way, and from her we learned also to be brave and prompt in time of danger, and not to run away, but face the peril that threatened friend or stranger, and help him the best we could without stopping to think what the cost might be to us. And she taught us not by words only, but by example, and that is the best way and the surest and the most lasting. Why, the brave things she did, the splendid things! she was just a soldier; and so modest about it—well, you couldn't help admiring her, and you couldn't help imitating her; not even a King Charles spaniel could remain entirely despicable in her society. So, as you see, there was more to her than her education.

CHAPTER 2

When I was well grown, at last, I was sold and taken away, and I never saw her again. She was broken-hearted, and so was I, and we cried; but she comforted me as well as she could, and said we were sent into this world for a wise and good purpose, and must do our duties without repining, take our life as we might find it, live it for the best good of others, and never mind about the results; they were not our affair. She said men who did like this would have a noble and beautiful reward by and by in another world, and although we animals would not go there, to do well and right without reward would give to our brief lives a worthiness and dignity which in itself would be a reward. She had gathered these things from time to time when she had gone to the Sunday-school with the children, and had laid them up in her memory more carefully than she had done with those other words and phrases; and she had studied them deeply, for her good and ours. One may see by this that she had a wise and thoughtful head, for all there was so much lightness and vanity in it.

So we said our farewells, and looked our last upon each other through our tears; and the last thing she said—keeping it for the last to make me remember it the better, I think—was, "In memory of me, when there is a time of danger to another do not think of yourself, think of your mother, and do as she would do."

Do you think I could forget that? No.

CHAPTER 3

It was such a charming home!—my new one; a fine great house, with pictures, and delicate decorations, and rich furniture, and no gloom anywhere, but all the wilderness of dainty colors lit up with flooding sunshine; and the spacious grounds around it, and the great garden—oh, greensward, and noble trees, and flowers, no end! And I was the same as a member of the family; and they loved me, and petted me, and did not give me a new name, but called me by my old one that was dear to me because my mother had given it me—Aileen Mavourneen. She got it out of a song; and the Grays knew that song, and said it was a beautiful name.

Mrs. Gray was thirty, and so sweet and so lovely, you cannot imagine it; and Sadie was ten, and just like her mother, just a darling slender little copy of her, with auburn tails down her back, and short frocks; and the baby was a year old, and plump and dimpled, and fond of me, and never could get enough of hauling on my tail, and hugging me, and laughing out its innocent happiness; and Mr. Gray was thirty-eight, and tall and slender and handsome, a little bald in front, alert, quick in his movements, business-like, prompt, decided, unsentimental, and with that kind of trim-chiseled face that just seems to glint and sparkle with frosty intellectuality! He was a renowned scientist. I do not know what the word means, but my mother would know how to use it and get effects. She would know how to depress a rat-terrier with it and make a lap-dog look sorry he came. But that is not the best one; the best one was Laboratory. My mother could organize a Trust on that one that would skin the tax-collars off the whole herd. The laboratory was not a book, or a picture, or a place to wash your hands in, as the college president's dog said—no, that is the lavatory; the laboratory is quite different, and is filled with jars, and bottles, and electrics, and wires, and strange machines; and every week other scientists came there and sat in the place, and used the machines, and discussed, and made what they called experiments and discoveries; and often I came, too, and stood around and listened, and tried to learn, for the sake of my mother, and in loving memory of her, although it was a pain to me, as realizing what she was losing out of her life and I gaining nothing at all; for try as I might, I was never able to make anything out of it at all.

Other times I lay on the floor in the mistress's work-room and slept, she gently using me for a foot-stool, knowing it pleased me, for it was a caress; other times I spent an hour in the nursery, and got well tousled and made happy; other times I watched by the crib there, when the baby was asleep and the nurse out for a few minutes on the baby's affairs; other times I romped and raced through the grounds and the garden with Sadie till we were tired out, then slumbered on the grass in the shade of a tree while she read her book; other times I went visiting among the neighbor dogs—for there were some most pleasant ones not far away, and one very handsome and

W. T. SMEDLEY, *A DOG'S TALE*, 1904, PAGE 18

courteous and graceful one, a curly-haired Irish setter by the name of Robin Adair, who was a Presbyterian like me, and belonged to the Scotch minister.

The servants in our house were all kind to me and were fond of me, and so, as you see, mine was a pleasant life. There could not be a happier dog than I was, nor a gratefuler one. I will say this for myself, for it is only the truth: I tried in all ways to do well and right, and honor my mother's memory and her teachings, and earn the happiness that had come to me, as best I could.

By and by came my little puppy, and then my cup was full, my happiness was perfect. It was the dearest little waddling thing, and so smooth and soft and velvety, and had such cunning little awkward paws, and such affectionate eyes, and such a sweet and innocent face; and it made me so proud to see how the children and their mother adored it, and fondled it, and exclaimed over every little wonderful thing it did. It did seem to me that life was just too lovely to—

Then came the winter. One day I was standing a watch in the nursery. That is to say, I was asleep on the bed. The baby was asleep in the crib, which was alongside the bed, on the side next the fireplace. It was the kind of crib that has a lofty tent over it made of a gauzy stuff that you can see through. The nurse was out, and we two sleepers were alone. A spark from the wood-fire was shot out, and it lit on the slope of the tent. I suppose a quiet interval followed, then a scream from the baby woke me, and there was that tent flaming up toward the ceiling! Before I could think, I sprang to the floor in my fright, and in a second was half-way to the door; but in the next half-second my mother's farewell was sounding in my ears, and I was back on the bed again. I reached my head through the flames and dragged the baby out by the waist-band, and tugged it along, and we fell to the floor together in a cloud of smoke; I snatched a new hold, and dragged the screaming little creature along and out at the door and around the bend of the hall, and was still tugging away, all excited and happy and proud, when the master's voice shouted:

"Begone, you cursed beast!" and I jumped to save myself; but he was wonderfully quick, and chased me up, striking furiously at me with his cane, I dodging this way and that, in terror, and at last a strong blow fell upon my left foreleg, which made me shriek and fall, for the moment, helpless; the cane went up for another blow, but never descended, for the nurse's voice rang wildly out, "The nursery's on fire!" and the master rushed away in that direction, and my other bones were saved.

The pain was cruel, but, no matter, I must not lose any time; he might come back at any moment; so I limped on three legs to the other end of the hall, where there was a dark little stairway leading up into a garret where old boxes and such things were kept, as I had heard say, and where people seldom went. I managed to climb up there, then I searched my way through the dark among the piles of things, and hid in the secretest place I could find. It was foolish to be afraid there, yet still I was; so afraid that I held in and hardly even whimpered, though it would have been such a comfort to whimper, because that eases the pain, you know. But I could lick my leg, and that did me some good.

For half an hour there was a commotion downstairs, and shoutings, and rushing footsteps, and then there was quiet again. Quiet for some minutes, and that was grateful to my spirit, for then my fears began to go down; and fears are worse than pains—oh, much worse. Then came a sound that froze me. They were calling me—calling me by name—hunting for me!

It was muffled by distance, but that could not take the terror out of it, and it was the most dreadful sound to me that I had ever heard. It went all about, everywhere, down there: along the halls, through all the rooms, in both stories, and in the basement and the cellar; then outside, and farther and farther away—then back, and all about the house again, and I thought it would never, never stop. But at last it did, hours and hours after the vague twilight of the garret had long ago been blotted out by black darkness.

Then in that blessed stillness my terrors fell little by little away, and I was at peace and slept. It was a good rest I had, but I woke before the twilight had come again. I was feeling fairly comfortable, and I could think out a plan now. I made a very good one; which was, to creep down, all the way down the back stairs, and hide behind the cellar door, and slip out and escape when the iceman came at dawn, while he was inside filling the refrigerator; then I would hide all day, and start on my journey when night came; my journey to—well, anywhere where they would not know me and betray me to the master. I was feeling almost cheerful now; then suddenly I thought: Why, what would life be without my puppy!

That was despair. There was no plan for me; I saw that; I must stay where I was; stay, and wait, and take what might come—it was not my affair; that was what life is—my mother had said it. Then—well, then the calling began again! All my sorrows came back. I said to myself, the master will never forgive. I did not know what I had done to make him so bitter and so unforgiving, yet I judged it was something a dog could not understand, but which was clear to a man and dreadful.

They called and called—days and nights, it seemed to me. So long that the hunger and thirst near drove me mad, and I recognized that I was getting very weak. When you are this way you sleep a great deal, and I did. Once I woke in an awful fright—it seemed to me that the calling was right there in the garret! And so it was: it was Sadie's voice, and she was crying; my name was falling from her lips all broken, poor thing, and I could not believe my ears for the joy of it when I heard her say:

W. T. SMEDLEY, *A DOG'S TALE*, 1904, PAGE 28

"Come back to us—oh, come back to us, and forgive—it is all so sad without our—"

I broke in with such a grateful little yelp, and the next moment Sadie was plunging and stumbling through the darkness and the lumber and shouting for the family to hear, "She's found, she's found!"

The days that followed—well, they were wonderful. The mother and Sadie and the servants—why, they just seemed to worship me. They couldn't seem to make me a bed that was fine enough; and as for food, they couldn't be satisfied with anything but game and delicacies that were out of season; and every day the friends and neighbors flocked in to hear about my heroism—that was the name they called it by, and it means agriculture. I remember my mother pulling it on a kennel once, and explaining it that way, but didn't say what agriculture was, except that it was synonymous with intramural incandescence; and a dozen times a day Mrs. Gray and Sadie would tell the tale to new-comers, and say I risked my life to save the baby's, and both of us had burns to prove it, and then the company would pass me around and pet me and exclaim about me, and you could see the pride in the eyes of Sadie and her mother; and when the people wanted to know what made me limp, they looked ashamed and changed the subject, and sometimes when people hunted them this way and that way with questions about it, it looked to me as if they were going to cry.

And this was not all the glory; no, the master's friends came, a whole twenty of the most distinguished people, and had me in the laboratory, and discussed me as if I was kind of discovery; and some of them said it was wonderful in a dumb beast, the finest exhibition of instinct they could call to mind; but the master said, with vehemence, "It's far above instinct; it's reason, and many a man, privileged to be saved and go with you and me to a better world by right of its possession, has less of it than this poor silly quadruped that's foreordained to perish"; and then he laughed, and said: "Why, look at me—I'm a sarcasm! bless you, with all my grand intelligence, the only thing I inferred was that the dog had gone mad and was destroying the child, whereas but for the beast's intelligence—it's reason, I tell you!—the child would have perished!"

They disputed and disputed, and I was the very center and subject of it all, and I wished my mother could know that this grand honor had come to me; it would have made her proud.

Then they discussed optics, as they called it, and whether a certain injury to the brain would produce blindness or not, but they could not agree about it, and said they must test it by experiment by and by; and next they discussed plants, and that interested me, because in the summer Sadie and I had planted seeds—I helped her dig the holes, you know—and after days and days a little shrub or a flower came up there, and it was a wonder how that could happen; but it did, and I wished I could talk—I would have told those people about it and shown them how much I knew, and been all alive with the subject; but I didn't care for the optics; it was dull, and when they came back to it again it bored me, and I went to sleep.

Pretty soon it was spring, and sunny and pleasant and lovely, and the sweet mother and the children patted me and the puppy good-by, and went away on a journey and a visit to their kin, and the master wasn't any company for us, but we played

W. T. SMEDLEY, *A DOG'S TALE*, 1904

together and had good times, and the servants were kind and friendly, so we got along quite happily and counted the days and waited for the family.

And one day those men came again, and said, now for the test, and they took the puppy to the laboratory, and I limped three-leggedly along, too, feeling proud, for any attention shown the puppy was a pleasure to me, of course. They discussed and experimented, and then suddenly the puppy shrieked, and they set him on the floor, and he went staggering around, with his head all bloody, and the master clapped his hands and shouted:

"There, I've won—confess it! He's as blind as a bat!"

And they all said:

"It's so—you've proved your theory, and suffering humanity owes you a great debt from henceforth," and they crowded around him, and wrung his hand cordially and thankfully, and praised him.

But I hardly saw or heard these things, for I ran at once to my little darling, and snuggled close to it where it lay, and licked the blood, and it put its head against mine, whimpering softly, and I knew in my heart it was a comfort to it in its pain and trouble to feel its mother's touch, though it could not see me. Then it dropped down, presently, and its little velvet nose rested upon the floor, and it was still, and did not move any more.

Soon the master stopped discussing a moment, and rang in the footman, and said, "Bury it in the far corner of the garden," and then went on with the discussion, and I trotted after the footman, very happy and grateful, for I knew the puppy was

W. T. SMEDLEY, *A DOG'S TALE*, 1904, PAGE 34

out of its pain now, because it was asleep. We went far down the garden to the farthest end, where the children and the nurse and the puppy and I used to play in the summer in the shade of a great elm, and there the footman dug a hole, and I saw he was going to plant the puppy, and I was glad, because it would grow and come up a fine handsome dog, like Robin Adair, and be a beautiful surprise for the family when they came home; so I tried to help him dig, but my lame leg was no good, being stiff, you know, and you have to have two, or it is no use. When the footman had finished and covered little Robin up, he patted my head, and there were tears in his eyes, and he said: "Poor little doggie, you saved his child."

I have watched two whole weeks, and he doesn't come up! This last week a fright has been stealing upon me. I think there is something terrible about this. I do not know what it is, but the fear makes me sick, and I cannot eat, though the servants bring me the best of food; and they pet me so, and even come in the night, and cry, and say, "Poor doggie—do give it up and come home; don't break our hearts!" and all this terrifies me the more, and makes me sure something has happened. And I am so weak; since yesterday I cannot stand on my feet any more. And within this hour the servants, looking toward the sun where it was sinking out of sight and the night chill coming on, said things I could not understand, but they carried something cold to my heart.

"Those poor creatures! They do not suspect. They will come home in the morning, and eagerly ask for the little doggie that did the brave deed, and who of us will be strong enough to say the truth to them: 'The humble little friend is gone where go the beasts that perish.'"

———••—•—••———

Despite its liberal sentimentality, A Dog's Tale *enjoyed considerable international success. England's National Anti-Vivisection Society arranged for a special edition of the book to be published for distribution among dog lovers at a moment when British opponents of vivisection were up in arms over a legal case concerning a university scientist who had experimented on a dog. In fact, it's possible Mark Twain's story was partly inspired by that case.*

According to a December 1903 newspaper story, a young girl was so taken by the magazine publication of A Dog's Tale *she wrote this brief letter to its author: "dear Mister Mark, I liked your doggy and the poor little puppie to. now pleas rite us a cats tail quick. your playmate jessie." (Jessie's original letter appears not to have survived. Mark Twain was in Italy at the time she wrote and may not have received it. Moreover, he saved little correspondence from his sojourns abroad.)*

———••—•—••———

E. W. KEMBLE, *MARK TWAIN'S LIBRARY OF HUMOR*, 1888, PAGE 404

PART IV.
PARTY ANIMALS

Few dogs found in Mark Twain's vast writings can be called truly vicious. Most are playful or simply harmless. Some are so much fun, in fact, they might justifiably be called "party animals."

Speaking of fun-loving animals . . . in his 1940 book *Mark Twain and I*, humorist Opie Read claimed to have overheard a conversation between Mark Twain and poet James Whitcomb Riley that touched on a dog's sense of humor. Riley reportedly said, "It seems to me that even a dog at times can see the funny side of things." To that, Mark Twain responded, "Certainly. Tell a dog a joke and he never fails to wag his tail. I had a dog that would wag himself from one side of the road to the other whenever I introduced him to a politician."

29.

THE POODLE VS.
THE PINCH BEETLE

Although neither Tom Sawyer nor Huck Finn owns a dog in any of Mark Twain's stories, dogs appear frequently throughout both Tom Sawyer and Huckleberry Finn—usually as friendly neighbors or tracking animals. The first mention of "dog" in Tom Sawyer comes in the book's second chapter, in which Tom's Aunt Polly orders him to whitewash an immense fence. In one of the most memorable scenes in children's literature, Tom persuades his friends to pay him for the privilege of doing his work. Among the loot he collects from that enterprise is a "dog collar—but no dog." He does get a live kitten, but it has only one eye. The cycloptic kitten is not heard from again, but Tom encounters a dog in church the following Sunday. This fun-loving animal helps shatter the tedium of the pastor's sermon. (Illustrations of that scene, incidentally, show the dog without a collar.)

ACHILLE SIROUY, *LES AVENTURES DE TOM SAWYER*, 1876, PAGE 39

Now [Tom] lapsed into suffering again, as the dry argument was resumed. Presently he bethought him of a treasure he had and got it out. It was a large black beetle with formidable jaws—a "pinch-bug," he called it. It was in a percussion-cap box. The first thing the beetle did was to take him by the finger. A natural fillip followed, the beetle went floundering into the aisle and lit on its back, and the hurt finger went into the boy's mouth. The beetle lay there working its helpless legs, unable to turn over. Tom eyed it, and longed for it; but it was safe out of his reach. Other people uninterested in the sermon, found relief in the beetle, and they eyed it too. Presently a vagrant poodle dog came idling along, sad at heart, lazy with the summer softness and the quiet, weary of captivity, sighing for change. He spied the beetle; the drooping tail lifted and wagged. He surveyed the prize; walked around it; smelt at it from a safe distance; walked around it again; grew bolder, and took a closer smell; then lifted his lip and made a gingerly snatch at it, just missing it; made another, and another; began to enjoy the diversion; subsided to his stomach with the beetle between his paws, and continued his experiments; grew weary at last, and then indifferent and absent-minded. His head nodded, and little by little his chin descended and touched the enemy, who seized it. There was a sharp yelp, a flirt of the poodle's head, and the beetle fell a couple of yards away, and lit on its back once more. The neighboring spectators shook with a gentle inward joy, several faces went behind fans and handkerchiefs, and Tom was entirely happy. The dog looked foolish, and probably felt so; but there was resentment in his heart, too, and a craving for revenge. So he went to the beetle and began a wary attack on it again; jumping at it from every point of a circle, lighting with his forepaws within an inch of the creature, making even closer snatches at it with his teeth, and jerking his head till his ears flapped again. But he grew tired once more, after a while; tried to amuse himself with a fly but found no relief; followed an ant around, with his nose close to the floor, and quickly wearied of that; yawned, sighed, forgot the beetle entirely, and sat down on it! Then there was a wild yelp of agony and the poodle went sailing up the aisle; the yelps continued, and so did the dog; he crossed the house in front of the altar; he flew down the other aisle; he crossed before the doors; he clamored up the home-stretch; his anguish grew with his progress, till presently he was but a woolly comet moving in its orbit with the gleam and the speed of light. At last the frantic sufferer sheered from its course, and sprang into its master's lap; he flung it out of the window, and the voice of distress quickly thinned away and died in the distance.

By this time the whole church was red-faced and suffocating with suppressed laughter, and the sermon had come to a dead stand-still. The discourse was resumed presently, but it went lame and halting, all possibility of impressiveness being at an end; for even the gravest sentiments were constantly being received with a smothered burst of unholy mirth, under cover of some remote pew-back, as if the poor parson had said a rarely facetious thing. It was a genuine relief to the whole congregation when the ordeal was over and the benediction pronounced.

Tom Sawyer went home quite cheerful, thinking to himself that there was some satisfaction about divine service when there was a bit of variety in it. He had but one marring thought; he was willing that the dog should play with his pinch-bug, but he did not think it was upright in him to carry it off.

Dogs have been named after Mark Twain. Horses have been named after him. Cats have been named after him. Even other people have been named after him. Now, a beetle has been named after him! In early 2016, Clemson University entomologist Michael L. Ferro announced his discovery of a brand-new California beetle species to which he gave the Latin name Sonoma twaini—*in honor of the man he regards as the "all-time greatest humorist." In a private communication, he told the editor of the present volume that Tom Sawyer's "pinch-bug" is probably a gangly and unwieldy stag beetle that would fit the novel's description well.*

30.

"AMEN" TO
THE HOWLING DOG

———————•◆•———————

Another dog disrupting a solemn service appears in Mark Twain's autobiographical dictations. Around the mid-1870s, his pastor friend Joe Twichell conducted a prayer service at a Civil War reunion gathering in Hartford's biggest church. Everything went fine until someone didn't look where he was stepping.

———————•◆•———————

The crowd massed themselves together around Twichell with uncovered heads, the silence and solemnity interrupted only by subdued sneezings, for these people were buried in the dim cloud of dust. After a pause Twichell began an impressive prayer, making it brief to meet the exigencies of the occasion. In the middle of it he made a pause. The drummer thought he was through, and let fly a rub-a-dub-dub—and the little Major stormed out "*Stop* that drum!"

Twichell tried again. He got almost to the last word safely, when somebody trod on a dog and the dog let out a howl of anguish that could be heard beyond the frontier. The Major said, "God damn that dog!"

—and Twichell said, "Amen."

That is, he said it as a finish to his own prayer, but it fell so exactly at the right moment that it seemed to include the Major's, too, and so he felt greatly honored, and thanked him.

31.

WHY DOGS AREN'T WELCOME
AT FUNERALS

———————————————

An unfinished burlesque of etiquette books that Mark Twain began around 1881 offers rules for proper behavior at funerals. For example, "At the moving passages, be moved—but only according to the degree of your intimacy with the parties giving the entertainment, or with the party in whose honor the entertainment is given. Where a blood relation sobs, an intimate friend should choke up, a distant relation should sigh, a stranger should merely fumble sympathetically with his handkerchief."

The burlesque's most valuable piece of advice, however, is simply this: "Do not bring your dog." Huck's description of Peter Wilks's funeral in Huckleberry Finn *below should help explain why not. The scene is a solemn one, a parlor crammed with mourners seated around the deceased's open casket. Aside from sobbing, "There warn't no other sound but the scraping of the feet on the floor, and blowing noses—because people always blow them more at a funeral than they do at other places except church."*

When the place was packed full, the undertaker he slid around in his black gloves with his softy soothering ways, putting on the last touches, and getting people and things all ship-shape and comfortable, and making no more sound than a cat. He never spoke; he moved people around, he squeezed in late ones, he opened up passage-ways, and done it all with nods, and signs with his hands. Then he took his place over against the wall. He was the softest, glidingest, stealthiest man I ever see; and there warn't no more smile to him than there is to a ham.

They had borrowed a melodeum—a sick one; and when everything was ready, a young woman set down and worked it, and it was pretty skreeky and colicky, and everybody joined in and sung, and Peter was the only one that had a good thing, according to my notion. Then the Reverend Hobson opened up, slow and solemn, and begun to talk; and straight off the most outrageous row busted out in the cellar a body ever heard; it was only one dog, but he made a most powerful racket, and he kept it up, right along; the parson he had to stand there, over the coffin, and wait—you couldn't hear yourself think. It was right down awkward, and nobody didn't seem to know what to do. But pretty soon they see that long-legged undertaker make a sign to the preacher as much as to say, "Don't you worry—

"HE HAD A RAT!"

E. W. KEMBLE, *HUCKLEBERRY FINN*, 1885, PAGE 233

just depend on me." Then he stooped down and begun to glide along the wall, just his shoulders showing over the people's heads. So he glided along, and the pow-wow and racket getting more and more outrageous all the time; and at last, when he had gone around two sides of the room, he disappears down cellar. Then, in about two seconds we heard a whack, and the dog he finished up with a most amazing howl or two, and then everything was dead still, and the parson begun his solemn talk where he left off. In a minute or two here comes this undertaker's back and shoulders gliding along the wall again; and so he glided, and glided, around three sides of the room, and then rose up, and shaded his mouth with his hands, and stretched his neck out towards the preacher, over the people's heads, and says, in a kind of a coarse whisper, "He had a rat!" Then he drooped down and glided along the wall again to his place. You could see it was a great satisfaction to the people, because naturally they wanted to know. A little thing like that don't cost nothing, and it's just the little things that makes a man to be looked up to and liked. There warn't no more popular man in town than what that undertaker was.

Entries in Mark Twain's private notebooks show he had wanted to find a literary use for the howling dog that had disrupted Joe Twichell's prayer in Hartford (see chapter 30). When he finally found that opportunity in the above passage in Huckleberry Finn, *its source did not go unnoticed. A Hartford newspaper pointed out that where the scene "actually occurred in this city, will be recognized by a number of Hartford people, who have had many hearty laughs at it in its chrysalis period."*

32.

HOUNDS LIKE SPOKES
OF A WHEEL

Huck's journey down the Mississippi River in Huckleberry Finn *ends with his finding himself alone in Arkansas and not knowing where his companion Jim is. By pure chance, he stumbles onto a farm owned by Tom Sawyer's Aunt Sally and Uncle Silas Phelps, who mistake him for Tom. Soon, the real Tom shows up, and tells Huck to continue pretending to be him, while he pretends to be his own half-brother, Sid. Like the farm of Mark Twain's real uncle, John Quarles (see chapter 1), on which the Phelps home is modeled, the latter is teeming with dogs.*

Phelps's was one of these little one-horse cotton plantations; and they all look alike. A rail fence round a two-acre yard; a stile, made out of logs sawed off and up-ended, in steps, like barrels of a different length, to climb

WORTH BREHM, *HUCKLEBERRY FINN*, HARPER, 1923, PAGE 314

over the fence with, and for the women to stand on when they are going to jump onto a horse; some sickly grass-patches in the big yard, but mostly it was bare and smooth, like an old hat with the nap rubbed off; big double log house for the white folks—hewed logs, with the chinks stopped up with mud or mortar, and these mud-stripes been whitewashed some time or another; round-log kitchen, with a big broad, open but roofed passage joining it to the house; log smoke-house back of the kitchen; three little log slave-cabins in a row t'other side the smokehouse; one little hut all by itself away down against the back fence, and some outbuildings down a piece the other side; ash-hopper, and big kettle to bile soap in, by the little hut; bench by the kitchen door, with bucket of water and a gourd; hound asleep there, in the sun; more hounds asleep, round about; about three shade-trees away off in a corner; some currant bushes and gooseberry bushes in one place by the fence; outside of the fence a garden and a water-melon patch; then the cotton fields begins; and after the fields, the woods.

I went around and clumb over the back stile by the ash-hopper, and started for the kitchen. When I got a little ways, I heard the dim hum of a spinning-wheel wailing along up and sinking along down again; and then I knowed for certain I wished I was dead—for that is the lonesomest sound in the whole world.

I went right along, not fixing up any particular plan, but just trusting to Providence to put the right words in my mouth when the time come; for I'd noticed that Providence always did put the right words in my mouth, if I left it alone.

When I got half-way, first one hound and then another got up and went for me, and of course I stopped and faced them, and kept still. And such another pow-wow as they made! In a quarter of a minute I was a kind of a hub of a wheel, as you may say—spokes made out of dogs—circle of fifteen of them packed together around me, with their necks and noses stretched up towards me, a barking and howling; and more a coming; you could see them sailing over fences and around corners from everywheres.

A slave woman come tearing out of the kitchen with a rolling-pin in her hand, singing out, "Begone! you Tige! you Spot! begone, sah!" and she fetched first one and then another of them a clip and sent him howling, and then the rest followed; and the next second, half of them come back, wagging their tails around me and making friends with me. There ain't no harm in a hound, nohow.

Huck and Tom encounter bloodhounds at the Phelps farm again in Tom Sawyer, Detective *(1896), in which Huck reaffirms his affection for them: "There ain't any dog that's got a lovelier disposition than a bloodhound . . ." Mark Twain later made a less pleasant use of bloodhounds in his novella* A Double-Barrelled Detective Story *published in 1902. That story begins with a man lashing his wife to a tree and turning vicious bloodhounds on her. The woman survives the attack to bear the man's son. When the boy grows up to have the instincts and tracking abilities of a bloodhound, his mother sends him to find his cruel father and exact revenge.*

33.

EVEN DOGS LOVE A PARADE

In the novel Pudd'nhead Wilson, *Italian twins of noble birth cause a sensation when they move into an obscure little Missouri town. In Mark Twain's earlier draft of the novel, titled "Those Extraordinary Twins," the Italian brothers cause an even greater sensation. In that story, the twins are* conjoined—*and not in any ordinary, run-of-the-mill Siamese-twin kind of way. They share a single torso and single pair of legs, while having separate heads and arms. The sight of such an unlikely combination of body parts naturally turns the heads of spectators—even dog spectators—when the twins are paraded through the town. Who wouldn't be dazzled by a human body with four arms and two heads?*

All along the streets the people crowded the windows and stared at the amazing twins. Troops of small boys flocked after the buggy, excited and yelling. At first the dogs showed no interest. They thought they merely saw three men in a buggy—a matter of no consequence; but when they found out the facts of the case, they altered their opinion pretty radically, and joined the boys, expressing their minds as they came. Other dogs got interested; indeed, all the dogs. It was a spirited sight to see them come leaping fences, tearing around corners, swarming out of every by-street and alley. The noise they made was something beyond belief—or praise. They did not seem to be moved by malice but only by prejudice, the common human prejudice against lack of conformity. If the twins turned their heads, they broke and fled in every direction, but stopped at a safe distance and faced about; and then formed and came on again as soon as the strangers showed them their back.

F. M. SENIOR, *PUDD'NHEAD WILSON & THOSE EXTRAORDINARY TWINS*, 1894, PAGE 347

W. F. BROWN, *A TRAMP ABROAD*, 1880, PAGE 48

PART V.

———•———

DOGS WITH FOREIGN ACCENTS

Mark Twain spent nearly twelve years of his life traveling and living outside the United States. His travels included extended stays in Hawaii—then an independent kingdom—England, France, Germany, Austria, Italy, Australia, India, South Africa, and other countries. With such diverse foreign experience, it should not be surprising that some of his most interesting observations about dogs concern animals he encountered while abroad.

34.

A PASSIONATE FONDNESS
FOR DOGS

———————

Mark Twain's first experience outside the United States and its continental territories was a four-month visit to Hawaii in 1866, when the future U.S. state was an independent kingdom known to the outside world as the Sandwich Islands. He was fascinated by the islands' Polynesian culture and monarchy, which he described in letters to a California newspaper and later in lectures with which he began his public speaking career. Of particular interest to him was the deep devotion to their dogs of native Hawaiians, whom he generally called "Kanakas."

———————

The Kanakas are passionately fond of dogs—not great, magnificent Newfoundlands or stately mastiffs or graceful greyhounds—but a species of little, puny, cowardly, sneaking, noisy cur that a white man would condemn to death on general principles. They love these puppies better than they love one another—better than their children or their religion. They feed them—stuff them—with poi and fish, from their own calabashes when the supply is scanty, and even the family must go hungry. They sleep with them; they don't mind the fleas. Men and women carry these dogs in their arms, always. If they have got to walk a mile, the dog must be carried—or five miles, for that matter—while the little children walk. The dog travels in the schooners with them.

I have seen a puppy hugged and caressed by a mother, and her little, tired, sore-footed child cuffed and slapped for stumbling to the ground and crying. When the woman rides on horseback, she often carries the puppy in front of her on the horse; and when the man rides—they nearly always go in a keen gallop—the puppy stands up behind the saddle, "thort-ships," as a sailor would say, and sways gently to and fro to the motion of the horse. No danger of its falling; it is educated to ride thus from earliest puppyhood. They passionately love and tenderly care for the puppy and feed it from their own hands until it is a full-grown dog—and then they cook it and eat it.

I did not eat any dog. I ate raw salt pork and poi, and that was bad enough, but I was lost in the woods and hungry.

35.

THE CELEBRATED SLUMPING DOGS OF CONSTANTINOPLE

Constantinople, the capital of the Ottoman Empire now known as Istanbul, has long been famous for its armies of stray dogs. At times, as many as 150,000 of the homeless creatures roamed the city streets. During the nineteenth century, the dogs were so celebrated they were a major tourist attraction in a city renowned for architectural splendors. When Mark Twain visited Constantinople in 1866, he wrote a letter to his family calling it "the handsomest city in the world." Despite his high opinion of the city's scenic wonders, however, he, too, was attracted by its famous dogs. As a modern travel writer has put it, "the characteristic of the city that marked it out from the rest of the world was the fact that it was an immense open air dog kennel."

The Innocents Abroad, *Mark Twain's highly embellished account of the* Quaker City *cruise that took him to the Mediterranean, repeatedly expresses his disappointments with the wonders of the Old World. Those disappointments unfortunately included*

Constantinople's dogs. It was the kind of disappointment one might express after looking forward to seeing Niagara Falls and finding their flow a mere trickle.

———————•———————

I am half willing to believe that the celebrated dogs of Constantinople have been misrepresented—slandered. I have always been led to suppose that they were so thick in the streets that they blocked the way; that they moved about in organized companies, platoons and regiments, and took what they wanted by determined and ferocious assault; and that at night they drowned all other sounds with their terrible howlings. The dogs I see here can not be those I have read of.

I find them every where, but not in strong force. The most I have found together has been about ten or twenty. And night or day a fair proportion of them were sound asleep. Those that were not asleep always looked as if they wanted to be. I never saw such utterly wretched, starving, sad-visaged, broken-hearted looking curs in my life. It seemed a grim satire to accuse such brutes as these of taking things by force of arms. They hardly seemed to have strength enough or ambition enough to walk across the street—I do not know that I have seen one walk that far yet. They are mangy and bruised and mutilated, and often you see one with the hair singed off him in such wide and well defined tracts that he looks like a map of the new Territories. They are the sorriest beasts that breathe— the most abject—the most pitiful. In their faces is a settled expression of melancholy, an air of hopeless despondency. The

GRAPHIC, 27 NOVEMBER 1886, PAGE 573; IMAGE OF MARK TWAIN IS FROM *INNOCENTS ABROAD* (1869), PAGE 566

hairless patches on a scalded dog are preferred by the fleas of Constantinople to a wider range on a healthier dog; and the exposed places suit the fleas exactly. I saw a dog of this kind start to nibble at a flea—a fly attracted his attention, and he made a snatch at him; the flea called for him once more, and that forever unsettled him; he looked sadly at his flea-pasture, then sadly looked at his bald spot. Then he heaved a sigh and dropped his head resignedly upon his paws. He was not equal to the situation.

The dogs sleep in the streets, all over the city. From one end of the street to the other, I suppose they will average about eight or ten to a block. Sometimes, of course, there are fifteen or twenty to a block. They do not belong to any body, and they seem to have no close personal friendships among each other. But they district the city themselves, and the dogs of each district, whether it be half a block in extent, or ten blocks, have to remain within its bounds. Woe to a dog if he crosses the line! His neighbors would snatch the balance of his hair off in a second. So it is said. But they don't look it.

They sleep in the streets these days. They are my compass— my guide. When I see the dogs sleep placidly on, while men, sheep, geese, and all moving things turn out and go around them, I know I am not in the great street where the hotel is, and must go further. In the Grand Rue the dogs have a sort of air of being on the lookout—an air born of being obliged to get out of the way of many carriages every day—and that expression one recognizes in a moment. It does not exist upon the face of any dog without the confines of that street. All others sleep placidly and keep no watch. They would not move, though the Sultan himself passed by.

In one narrow street (but none of them are wide) I saw three dogs lying coiled up, about a foot or two apart. End to end they lay, and so they just bridged the street neatly, from gutter to gutter. A drove of a hundred sheep came along. They stepped right over the dogs, the rear crowding the front, impatient to get on. The dogs looked lazily up, flinched a little when the impatient feet of the sheep touched their raw backs—sighed, and lay peacefully down again. No talk could be plainer than that. So some of the sheep jumped over them and others scrambled between, occasionally chipping a leg with their sharp hoofs, and when the whole flock had made the trip, the dogs sneezed a little, in the cloud of dust, but never budged their bodies an inch. I thought I was lazy, but I am a steam-engine compared to a Constantinople dog. But was not that a singular scene for a city of a million inhabitants?

These dogs are the scavengers of the city. That is their offi-
cial position, and a hard one it is. However, it is their protection. But for their usefulness in partially cleansing these terrible
streets, they would not be tolerated long. They eat any thing
and every thing that comes in their way, from melon rinds and
spoiled grapes up through all the grades and species of dirt and
refuse to their own dead friends and relatives—and yet they are
always lean, always hungry, always despondent. The people are
loath to kill them—do not kill them, in fact. The Turks have
an innate antipathy to taking the life of any dumb animal, it
is said. But they do worse. They hang and kick and stone and
scald these wretched creatures to the very verge of death, and
then leave them to live and suffer.

Once a Sultan proposed to kill off all the dogs here, and did
begin the work—but the populace raised such a howl of horror
about it that the massacre was stayed. After a while, he proposed to remove them all to an island in the Sea of Marmora.
No objection was offered, and a ship-load or so was taken away.
But when it came to be known that somehow or other the dogs
never got to the island, but always fell overboard in the night
and perished, another howl was raised and the transportation
scheme was dropped.

So the dogs remain in peaceable possession of the streets.
I do not say that they do not howl at night, nor that they do
not attack people who have not a red fez on their heads. I only
say that it would be mean for me to accuse them of these
unseemly things who have not seen them do them with my
own eyes or heard them with my own ears.

An article syndicated in American newspapers in 1913 chided Mark Twain for having called Constantinople's street dogs lazy because they didn't bother to rise from their naps when sheep marched over them. "He was mistaken," the article said, "they were not lazy. Their attitude was caused by a mournful and dignified submission to the inevitable. What was the good of getting up and lying down again a little further on, when there would be another procession of sheep in a few minutes?"

Mark Twain wasn't kidding about the sultan who had wanted to exterminate Constantinople's dogs. In fact, the government repeatedly tried to get rid of them, making its most serious effort in 1910. Reluctant simply to kill the dogs, Turkey's Muslim rulers instead had about 80,000 animals relocated to a tiny, barren island. As one would expect, terrible things happened to the dogs there. Meanwhile, an earthquake devastated Constantinople, and many Turks interpreted the disaster as divine retribution for the city's mistreatment of its dogs. Public protests over their expulsion grew so loud the government returned the surviving animals to Constantinople. In the 21st century, thousands of strays still roam the modern city's streets, but now the government works to vaccinate them against disease and has them neutered to limit their reproduction.

36.

GERMAN CORPS DOGS

———◆———

During the late 1870s, Mark Twain spent time in Heidelberg, Germany, where he got a close look at university student life. A Tramp Abroad, published in 1880, says a great deal about the student corps organized for social activities and for dueling. Dogs were an important part of the corps. The University of Heidelberg, incidentally, is a setting of the popular Sigmund Romberg operetta The Student Prince, *which was first produced during the 1920s.*

———◆———

It seemed to be a part of corps-etiquette to keep a dog or so, too. I mean a corps-dog—the common property of the organization, like the corps-steward or head servant; then there are other dogs, owned by individuals.

On a summer afternoon in the Castle gardens, I have seen six students march solemnly into the grounds, in single file, each carrying a bright Chinese parasol and leading a prodi-

W. F. BROWN, *A TRAMP ABROAD*, 1880, PAGE 48

gious dog by a string. It was a very imposing spectacle. Sometimes there would be about as many dogs around the pavilion
as students; and of all breeds and of all degrees of beauty and
ugliness. These dogs had a rather dry time of it; for they were
tied to the benches and had no amusement for an hour or two
at a time except what they could get out of pawing at the gnats,
or trying to sleep and not succeeding. However, they got a
lump of sugar occasionally—they were fond of that.

It seemed right and proper that students should indulge in
dogs; but everybody else had them, too,—old men and young
ones, old women and nice young ladies. If there is one spectacle that is unpleasanter than another, it is that of an elegantly
dressed young lady towing a dog by a string. It is said to be the
sign and symbol of blighted love. It seems to me that some
other way of advertising it might be devised, which would be
just as conspicuous and yet not so trying to the proprieties.

37.

A BARK THAT STABS
LIKE A KNIFE

In 1891, Mark Twain took his family to the French health resort Aix-les-Bains. He enjoyed almost everything about the beautiful retreat except its noises—especially those of barking dogs—in the neighborhood where his family roomed.

But just across the little narrow street is the little market square, and at a corner of that is that church that is neighbor to the Roman arch, and that narrow street, and that billiard-table of a market place, and that church are able, on a bet, to turn out more noise to the cubic yard at the wrong time than any other similar combination in the earth or out of it. In the street you have the skull-bursting thunder of the passing hack, a volume of sound not producible by six hacks anywhere else; on the hack is a lunatic with a whip,

HAROLD R. HEATON, "MARK TWAIN AT AIX-LES-BAINS," *CHICAGO DAILY TRIBUNE*, 8 NOVEMBER 1891

which he cracks to notify the public to get out of his way. This crack is as keen and sharp and penetrating and ear-splitting as a pistol shot at close range, and the lunatic delivers it in volleys, not single shots. You think you will not be able to live till he gets by, and when he does get by he only leaves a vacancy for the bandit who sells *Le Petit Journal* to fill with his strange and awful yell. He arrives with the early morning and the market people, and there is a dog that arrives at about the same time and barks steadily at nothing till he dies, and they fetch another dog just like him. The bark of this breed is the twin of the whip volley, and stabs like a knife. By and by, what is left of you the church-bell gets. There are many bells, and apparently 6,000 or 7,000 town clocks, and as they are all five minutes apart—probably by law—there are no intervals. Some of them are striking all the time—at least, after you go to bed they are. There is one clock that strikes the hour, and then strikes it over again to see if it was right. Then for evenings and Sundays there is a chime—a chime that starts in pleasantly and musically, then suddenly breaks into a frantic roar, and boom, and crash of warring sounds that make you think Paris is up and the revolution come again.

38.

"HAVING" A DOG IN ITALIAN

———————•——————

Mark Twain spent several years in Italy at different times. While there, he naturally tried to learn some of the local language—perhaps to make up for the deficiency he had experienced during his prospecting days at Jackass Hill (see chapter 6). Here he describes an instructional session on conjugating the Italian verb for "to have" that was conducted with military precision.

———————•——————

. . . the commander said the instruction drill would now begin, and asked for suggestions. I said: "They say *I have, thou hast, he has*, and so on, but they don't say *what*. It will be better, and more definite, if they have something to have; just an object, you know, a something—anything will do; anything that will give the listener a sort of personal as well as grammatical interest in their joys and complaints, you see."

He said: "It is a good point. Would a dog do?"

ALBERT LEVERING, "ITALIAN WITHOUT A MAS-
TER," *THE $30,000 BEQUEST & OTHER STORIES*, 1908,
PAGE 171

I said I did not know, but we could try a dog and see. So he sent out an aide-de-camp to give the order to add the dog.

The six privates of the Present Tense now filed in, in charge of Sergeant AVERE (*to have*), and displaying their banner. They formed in line of battle, and recited, one at a time, thus:

"*Io ho un cane*, I have a dog."

"*Tu hai un cane*, thou hast a dog."

"*Egli ha un cane*, he has a dog."

"*Noi abbaiamo un cane*, we have a dog."

"*Voi avete un cane*, you have a dog."

"*Eglino hanno un cane*, they have a dog."

No comment followed. They returned to camp, and I reflected a while. The commander said: "I fear you are disappointed."

"Yes," I said; "they are too monotonous, too singsong, too dead-and-alive; they have no expression, no elocution. It isn't natural; it could never happen in real life. A person who had just acquired a dog is either blame' glad or blame' sorry. He is not on the fence. I never saw a case. What the nation do you suppose is the matter with these people?"

He thought maybe the trouble was with the dog. He said: "These are *contadini* [farmers], you know, and they have a prejudice against dogs—that is, against marimane. Marimana dogs stand guard over people's vines and olives, you know, and are very savage, and thereby a grief and an inconvenience to persons who want other people's things at night. In my judgment they have taken this dog for a marimana, and have soured on him."

I saw that the dog was a mistake, and not functionable: we must try something else; something, if possible, that could evoke sentiment, interest, feeling.

"What is cat, in Italian?" I asked.

"Gatto."

"Is it a gentleman cat, or a lady?"

"Gentleman cat."

"How are these people as regards that animal?"

"We-ll, they—they—"

"You hesitate: that is enough. How are they about chickens?"

He tilted his eyes towards heaven in mute ecstasy. I understood.

39.

LOVE AMONG THE RUINS

———————•———————

In early 1892, Mark Twain wrote from Italy to his close friend the Protestant pastor Joe Twichell. His letter related an incident involving fierce guard dogs in the ancient and beautiful Campagna region surrounding Rome. One can only wonder what amused Mark Twain more—teasing the Reverend Joe with a mildly indecent story or twitting him about Protestant-Catholic differences.

———————•———————

The dogs of the Campagna (they watch sheep without human assistance) are big & warlike & are terrible creatures to meet in those lonely expanses. Two young Englishmen—one of them a friend of mine—were away out there yesterday, with a peasant guide of the region who is a simple-hearted & very devout Roman Catholic. At one point the guide stopped, & said they were now approaching a spot where two especially ferocious dogs were accustomed to herd

ARTIST UNKNOWN, *A TRAMP ABROAD*, 1880, PAGE 566

sheep; that it would be well to go cautiously & be prepared to retreat if they saw the dogs. So then they started on, but presently came suddenly upon the dogs. The immense brutes came straight for them, with death in their eyes. The guide said in a voice of horror, "Turn your backs, but for God's sake don't stir—I will pray—I will pray the Virgin to do a miracle & save us; she will hear me, oh, my God she surely will." And straightway he began to pray. The Englishmen stood quaking with fright, & wholly without faith in the man's prayer. But all at once the furious snarling of the dogs ceased—at three steps distant—& there was dead silence. After a moment my friend, who could no longer endure the awful suspense, turned—& there was the miracle, sure enough: the gentleman dog had mounted the lady dog & both had forgotten their solemn duty in the ecstasy of a higher interest!

The strangers were saved, & they retired from that place with thankful hearts. The guide was in a frenzy of pious gratitude

& exultation, & praised & glorified the Virgin without stint; & finally wound up with "But you—you are Protestants; she would not have done it for you; she did it for me—only me—praised be she forever more! & I will hang a picture of it in the church & it shall-be another proof that her loving care is still with her children who humbly believe & adore."

By the time the dogs got unattached the men were five miles from there.

40.

"DOG" IN GERMAN

———————————◆———————————

Mark Twain spent considerable time in Germany and Austria, so it is not surprising German was the foreign language he came closest to mastering. However, although he revered the German people and their culture, he couldn't resist poking fun at elements in their language that differed sharply from their English counterparts. In an appendix to A Tramp Abroad *titled "The Awful German Language," he used the German word for "dog" to point out what he regarded as an absurdity of German nouns.*

———————————◆———————————

The inventor of the language seems to have taken pleasure in complicating it in every way he could think of. For instance, if one is casually referring to a house, *Haus,* or a horse, *Pferd,* or a dog, *Hund,* he spells these words as I have indicated; but if he is referring to them in the Dative case, he sticks on a foolish and unnecessary *e* and spells them

Hause, Pferde, Hunde. So, as an added *e* often signifies the plural, as the *s* does with us, the new student is likely to go on for a month making twins out of a Dative dog before he discovers his mistake; and on the other hand, many a new student who could ill afford [the] loss, has bought and paid for two dogs and only got one of them, because he ignorantly bought that dog in the Dative singular when he really supposed he was talking plural, which left the law on the seller's side, of course, by the strict rules of grammar, and therefore a suit for recovery could not lie.

41.

LOADED FOR BEAR

———••—•—••———

In 1899, Mark Twain wrote a letter from Austria to his friend William Dean Howells, in which he delicately described an embarrassing incident he had just witnessed on a Vienna street. His reaction to that incident confirms what he had earlier stated in a Pudd'nhead Wilson maxim written for Following the Equator: *"Man is the Only Animal that Blushes. Or needs to."*

———••—•—••———

I was out walking at noon today, in splendid summer weather, & came dreaming around the corner of a palace, & found myself fenced off by a long leather strap; I traced the strap leftward & found a sweet young lady holding the end of it; I traced it to starboard, then, & found a prodigious dog hitched to that end. He probably thought it was his place, for he had one leg up & was washing it down. I was embarrassed, but those others were not. I waited a second

or two, not knowing just what to do, then backed away &
pulled out around the Fräulein & departed. She & the string
were barring the whole sidewalk. I went a little piece, then
stopped to observe. That dog was loaded for bear; & before
he had accomplished his relief, a woman, a boy, then a man,
then another man, had all been obliged to turn out & deploy
around the young lady. They ought to water that dog at home.
It would have made a curious picture if I had had a Kodak &
courage enough to use it. I felt a good deal of resentment
against that girl for making me do all the blushing & embarrassing by myself, there before the public, when by rights it
was her place to do it.

42.

AN UNSUITABLE DOG FOR ELEPHANT HUNTING?

———————•———————

While continuing his world lecture tour through India in 1896, Mark Twain encountered an unusual dog that moved him to write the passage that follows here. In claiming not to know what kind of dog he is describing, he is obviously pulling our legs, which, incidentally, are doubtless much longer than those of the dog in question.

———————•———————

I n the train, during a part of the return journey from Baroda, we had the company of a gentleman who had with him a remarkable looking dog. I had not seen one of its kind before, as far as I could remember; though of course I might have seen one and not noticed it, for I am not acquainted with dogs, but only with cats. This dog's coat was smooth and shiny and black, and I think it had tan trimmings around the edges of the dog, and perhaps underneath. It was a

FOLLOWING THE EQUATOR, 1897, PAGE 413

long, low dog, with very short, strange legs—legs that curved inboard, something like parentheses turned the wrong way (. Indeed, it was made on the plan of a bench for length and lowness. It seemed to be satisfied, but I thought the plan poor, and structurally weak, on account of the distance between the forward supports and those abaft. With age the dog's back was likely to sag; and it seemed to me that it would have been a stronger and more practicable dog if it had had some more legs. It had not begun to sag yet, but the shape of the legs showed that the undue weight imposed upon them was beginning to tell. It had a long nose, and floppy ears that hung down, and a resigned expression of countenance. I did not like to ask what kind of a dog it was, or how it came to be deformed, for it was plain that the gentleman was very fond of it, and naturally he could be sensitive about it. From delicacy I thought it best not to seem to notice it too much. No doubt a man with a dog like that feels just as a person does who has a child that is out of true. The gentleman was not merely fond of the dog, he was also proud of it—just the same, again, as a mother feels about her child when it is an idiot. I could see that he was proud of it, notwithstanding it was such a long dog and looked so resigned and pious. It had been all over the world with him, and had been pilgriming like that for years and years. It had traveled 50,000 miles by sea and rail, and had ridden in front of him on his horse 8,000. It had a silver medal from the Geographical Society of Great Britain for its travels, and I saw it. It had won prizes in dog shows, both in India and in England—I saw them. He said its pedigree was on record in the Kennel Club, and that it was a well-known dog. He said a great many people in London could recognize it the moment they saw it. I did not say anything, but I did not think it anything strange; I should know that dog again, myself, yet I am not careful about noticing dogs. He said that when he walked along in London, people often stopped and looked at the dog. Of course I did not say anything, for I did not want to hurt his feelings, but I could have explained to him that if you take a great long low dog like that and waddle it along the street anywhere in the world and not charge anything, people will stop and look. He was gratified because the dog took prizes. But that was nothing; if I were built like that I could take prizes myself. I wished I knew what kind of a dog it was, and what it was for, but I could not very well ask, for that would show that I did not know. Not that I want a dog like that, but only to know the secret of its birth.

I think he was going to hunt elephants with it, because I know, from remarks dropped by him, that he has hunted large game in India and Africa, and likes it. But I think that if he tries to hunt elephants with it, he is going to be disappointed. I do not believe that it is suited for elephants. It lacks energy, it lacks force of character, it lacks bitterness. These things all show in the meekness and resignation of its expression. It would not attack an elephant, I am sure of it. It might not run if it saw one coming, but it looked to me like a dog that would sit down and pray.

I wish he had told me what breed it was, if there are others; but I shall know the dog next time, and then if I can bring myself to it I will put delicacy aside and ask.

Mark Twain later made a similar joke when he drew a picture of the rear half of a dachshund and claimed not to know what kind of

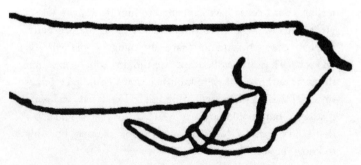

MARK TWAIN, "INSTRUCTIONS IN ART," *EUROPE & ELSEWHERE*, 1923, PAGE 323

dog it was because "the front end of it went around a corner before I could get to it." Meanwhile, his *Following the Equator anecdote* about the sausage dog moved him immediately to segue to the dog anecdote in chapter 48, below.

———————————

Mark Twain vacationing in Bermuda in 1908. Letters from his trips mention dogs he befriended in Bermuda, but the dog in this picture—which appears to be a pit bull—does not match their descriptions. It's certainly not the "lap dog" he mentions in one letter.

MARK TWAIN HOUSE AND MUSEUM, HARTFORD, CONNECTICUT

PART VI.

---·---

LESSONS WE CAN
LEARN FROM DOGS

Mark Twain's writings about dogs aren't all fun and games. As the selections in this part reveal, they also make points about what we can learn from the animals. Of course, because they come from Mark Twain, some of these lessons are still fun.

One lesson pertains to the famous aphorism "Let sleeping dogs lie." Its point, obviously, is the value of being content to leave well enough alone. Mark Twain apparently liked that aphorism but suggested modifying it. In one of the Pudd'nhead Wilson maxims he affixed to chapter heads in *Following the Equator*, he wrote, "The old saw says, 'Let a sleeping dog lie.' Right. Still, when there is much at stake it is better to get a newspaper to do it." A decade later, he modified his view in a letter to a friend: "'Let a sleeping dog lie.' It is a poor old maxim, & nothing in it; anybody can do it, you don't have to employ a dog."

43.

BENEVOLENCE AND
ITS REWARDS

If ever Mark Twain composed a persuasive cautionary tale, this is it. He hated sham piety and questioned the sincerity of altruistic do-gooders. In this tale, a dog teaches a physician an indelible lesson about the dangers of doing good. Mark Twain must have meant it when he wrote, "It is very wearing to be good," in Life on the Mississippi. *He also repeatedly said, "Be good and you will be lonesome." To that, he might have added ". . . or dead."*

All my life, from boyhood up, I have had the habit of reading a certain set of anecdotes, written in the quaint vein of The World's ingenious Fabulist, for the lesson they taught me and the pleasure they gave me. They lay always convenient to my hand, and whenever I thought meanly of my kind I turned to them, and they banished that

EXTRACTED FROM MAUD HUMPHREY'S "WOUNDED COMRADES," 1898, COURTESY
LIBRARY OF CONGRESS

sentiment; whenever I felt myself to be selfish, sordid, and
ignorable I turned to them, and they told me what to do to win
back my self-respect. Many times I wished that the charming
anecdotes had not stopped with their happy climaxes, but had
continued the pleasing history of the several benefactors and
beneficiaries. This wish rose in my breast so persistently that
at last I determined to satisfy it by seeking out the sequels of
those anecdotes myself. So I set about it, and after great labor

and tedious research accomplished my task. I will lay the result before you, giving you each anecdote in its turn, and following it with its sequel as I gathered it through my investigations.

THE GRATEFUL POODLE

One day a benevolent physician (who had read the books) having found a stray poodle suffering from a broken leg, conveyed the poor creature to his home, and after setting and bandaging the injured limb gave the little outcast its liberty again, and thought no more about the matter. But how great was his surprise, upon opening his door one morning, some days later, to find the grateful poodle patiently waiting there, and in its company another stray dog, one of whose legs, by some accident, had been broken. The kind physician at once relieved the distressed animal, nor did he forget to admire the inscrutable goodness and mercy of God, who had been willing to use so humble an instrument as the poor outcast poodle for the inculcating of, etc., etc., etc.

SEQUEL

The next morning the benevolent physician found the two dogs, beaming with gratitude, waiting at his door, and with them two other dogs,—cripples. The cripples were speedily healed, and the four went their way, leaving the benevolent physician more overcome by pious wonder than ever. The day passed, the morning came. There at the door sat now the four reconstructed dogs, and with them four others requiring reconstruction. This day also passed, and another morning came; and now sixteen dogs, eight of them newly crippled, occupied the sidewalk, and the people were going around. By noon the broken legs were all set, but the pious wonder in the good physician's breast was beginning to get mixed with involuntary profanity. The sun rose once more, and exhibited thirty-two dogs, sixteen of them with broken legs, occupying the sidewalk and half of the street; the human spectators took up the rest of the room. The cries of the wounded, the songs of the healed brutes, and the comments of the on-looking citizens made great and inspiring cheer, but traffic was interrupted in that street. The good physician hired a couple of assistant surgeons and got through his benevolent work before dark, first taking the precaution to cancel his church membership, so that he might express himself with the latitude which the case required.

But some things have their limits. When once more the morning dawned, and the good physician looked out upon a massed and far-reaching multitude of clamorous and beseeching dogs, he said, "I might as well acknowledge it, I have been fooled by the books; they only tell the pretty part of the story, and then stop. Fetch me the shot-gun; this thing has gone along far enough."

He issued forth with his weapon, and chanced to step upon the tail of the original poodle, who promptly bit him in the leg. Now the great and good work which this poodle had been engaged in had engendered in him such a mighty and augmenting enthusiasm as to turn his weak head at last and drive him mad. A month later, when the benevolent physician lay in the death throes of hydrophobia, he called his weeping friends about him, and said—

"Beware of the books. They tell but half of the story. Whenever a poor wretch asks you for help, and you feel a doubt as to what result may flow from your benevolence, give yourself the benefit of the doubt and kill the applicant."

And so saying he turned his face to the wall and gave up the ghost.

44.

HOW A ST. BERNARD
SAVED THE DAY

———••••———

Mark Twain claimed to have no head for mathematics, but statistics fascinated him, and he loved collecting them. He once even said, "Statistics are more precious and useful than any other one thing in this world, except whisky—I mean hymnbooks." Doubtless he meant that—especially the part about whisky—I mean hymnbooks—as this next tale demonstrates. This passage immediately follows the last sentence of chapter 42.

———••••———

I f I seem strangely interested in dogs, I have a reason for it; for a dog saved me from an embarrassing position once, and that has made me grateful to these animals; and if by study I could learn to tell some of the kinds from the others, I should be greatly pleased. I only know one kind apart, yet, and that is the kind that saved me that time. I always know that kind when I meet it, and if it is hungry or lost I take care of it. The matter happened in this way:

It was years and years ago. I had received a note from Mr. Augustin Daly of the Fifth Avenue Theater, asking me to call the next time I should be in New York. I was writing plays, in those days, and he was admiring them and trying to get me a chance to get them played in Siberia. I took the first train—the early one—the one that leaves Hartford at 8.29 in the morning. At New Haven I bought a paper, and found it filled with glaring display—lines about a "bench-show" there. I had often heard of bench-shows, but had never felt any interest in them, because I supposed they were lectures that were not well attended. It turned out, now, that it was not that, but a dog-show. There was a double-leaded column about the king-feature of this one, which was called a Saint Bernard, and was worth $10,000, and was known to be the largest and finest of his species in the world. I read all this with interest, because out of my school-boy readings I dimly remembered how the priests and pilgrims of St. Bernard used to go out in the storms and dig these dogs out of the snowdrifts when lost and exhausted, and give them brandy and save their lives, and drag them to the monastery and restore them with gruel.

Also, there was a picture of this prize-dog in the paper, a noble great creature with a benignant countenance, standing by a table. He was placed in that way so that one could get a right idea of his great dimensions. You could see that he was just a shade higher than the table—indeed, a huge fellow for a dog. Then there was a description which went into the details. It gave his enormous weight—150½ pounds, and his length—4

C. ALLAN GILBERT, *FOLLOWING THE EQUATOR*, 1897, PAGE 423

feet 2 inches, from stem to stern-post; and his height—3 feet 1 inch, to the top of his back. The pictures and the figures so impressed me, that I could see the beautiful colossus before me, and I kept on thinking about him for the next two hours; then I reached New York, and he dropped out of my mind.

———————◆———————

After a lengthy account of his difficulties getting past a giant Irish-man guarding access to see Mr. Daly, Mark Twain figured he was sunk when the Irishman asked him if he was in show business.

———————◆———————

A fatal question. I recognized that I was defeated. If I answered no, he would cut the matter short and wave me to the door without the grace of a word—I saw it in his uncompromising eye; if I said I was a lecturer, he would despise me, and dismiss me with opprobrious words; if I said I was a dramatist, he would throw me out of the window. I saw that my case was hopeless, so I chose the course which seemed least humiliating: I would pocket my shame and glide out without answering. The silence was growing lengthy.

"I'll ask ye again. Are ye in the show business yerself?"

"Yes!"

I said it with splendid confidence; for in that moment the very twin of that grand New Haven dog loafed into the room, and I saw that Irishman's eye light eloquently with pride and affection.

"Ye are? And what is it?"

"I've got a bench-show in New Haven."

The weather *did* change then.

"You don't *say*, sir! And that's *your* show, sir! Oh, it's a grand show, it's a wonderful show, sir, and a proud man I am to see your honor this day. And ye'll be an expert, sir, and ye'll know all about dogs—more than ever they know theirselves, I'll take me oath to ut."

I said, with modesty: "I believe I have some reputation that way. In fact, my business requires it."

"Ye have *some* reputation, your honor! Bedad I believe you! There's not a jintleman in the worrld that can lay over ye in the judgmint of a dog, sir. Now I'll vinture that your honor'll know that dog's dimensions there better than he knows them his own self, and just by the casting of your educated eye upon him. Would you mind giving a guess, if ye'll be so good?"

I knew that upon my answer would depend my fate. If I made this dog bigger than the prize-dog, it would be bad diplomacy, and suspicious; if I fell too far short of the prize-dog, that would be equally damaging. The dog was standing by the table, and I believed I knew the difference between him and the one whose picture I had seen in the newspaper to a shade. I spoke promptly up and said: "It's no trouble to guess this noble creature's figures: height, three feet; length, four feet and three-quarters of an inch; weight, a hundred and forty-eight and a quarter."

The man snatched his hat from its peg and danced on it with joy, shouting: "Ye've hardly missed it the hair's breadth, hardly the shade of a shade, your honor! Oh, it's the miraculous eye ye've got, for the judgmint of a dog!"

And still pouring out his admiration of my capacities, he snatched off his vest and scoured off one of the wooden chairs with it, and scrubbed it and polished it, and said: "There, sit down, your honor, I'm ashamed of meself that I forgot ye were standing all this time; and do put on your hat, ye mustn't take cold, it's a drafty place; and here is your cigar, sir, a getting cold, I'll give ye a light. There. The place is all yours, sir, and if ye'll just put your feet on the table and make yourself at home, I'll stir around and get a candle and light ye up the ould crazy stairs and see that ye don't come to anny harm, for be this time Mr. Daly'll be that impatient to see your honor that he'll be taking the roof off."

He conducted me cautiously and tenderly up the stairs, lighting the way and protecting me with friendly warnings, then pushed the door open and bowed me in and went his way, mumbling hearty things about my wonderful eye for points of a dog. Mr. Daly was writing and had his back to me. He glanced over his shoulder presently, then jumped up and said: "Oh, dear me, I forgot all about giving instructions. I was just writing you to beg a thousand pardons. But how is it you are here? How did you get by that Irishman? You are the first man that's done it in five and twenty years. You didn't bribe him, I know that; there's not money enough in New York to do it. And you didn't persuade him; he is all ice and iron: there isn't a soft place nor a warm one in him anywhere. What is your secret? Look here; you owe me a hundred dollars for unintentionally giving you a chance to perform a miracle—for it is a miracle that you've done."

"That is all right," I said, "collect it of Jimmy Lewis."

That good dog not only did me that good turn in the time of my need, but he won for me the envious reputation among all the theatrical people from the Atlantic to the Pacific of being the only man in history who had ever run the blockade of Augustin Daly's back door.

———————————

This incident occurred—if it really did occur—sometime around the mid-1880s, when theater impresario Augustin Daly rejected Mark Twain's dramatization of Tom Sawyer. *In 1887, after Mark Twain attended a performance of William Shakespeare's* The Taming of the Shrew *at Daly's theater, he delivered a speech at a dinner party and gave a condensed version of the St. Bernard story. In that version, the only question the Irishman asked him was how much the dog weighed. By time he wrote* Following the Equator *a decade later, he had remembered—or invented—the dog's other dimensions.*

———————————

45.

MARK TWAIN TEACHES AN
AIREDALE A LESSON

The real Mark Twain may not have attended any dog shows before trying to see Augustin Daly, but a canine namesake of his would later become a bench-show star. In June 1916, Rhode Island real estate investor Thomas D. Higgins bought a three-year-old English bull terrier named "Mark Twain" for the purpose of competing in dog shows. The progeny of a sire named East Bank Tree Sauce and a dam named Pride of Providence, this handsome white dog already had an impressive bench-show resume when Higgins acquired him, and it would go on to even greater glory. While preparing the dog for new shows, Higgins said he was "confident that Mark Twain can prove that, although named after a humorist, the dogs which have been pitted against him will be unable to see the joke." After Mark Twain bagged numerous first prizes in several New England shows during the fall, his name came up again in an account of the big Providence, Rhode Island, show the following April.

COURTESY LIBRARY OF CONGRESS

P resident Thomas D. Higgins of the Kennel Club expected to win honors with his English bull terrier Mark Twain, who cleaned up all through New England last fall. Mark Twain showed that he was in fighting trim yesterday by gaining a decision over Cos Cob Consort, Charles Christensen's Airedale from North Troy, N.Y.

MARK TWAIN PROVES DISCIPLINARIAN

Cos Cob Consort was on his worst behavior all morning. He snarled and snapped at a poor whimpering little English bull terrier puppy that was stationed next to him until Mark Twain lost his patience entirely. He leaped right over the top of his stall and started a scrap that soon had every dog, from the tiniest Pekingese to the biggest Great Dane tugging at his leash to get into the fight. Mark Twain was finally separated from Cos Cob Consort and put back in his stall with a wire netting over the top to prevent any further clash. The precaution was unnecessary, however, for the Airedale had learned his lesson and was a good dog all day.

46.

MARK TWAIN MAKES A DOG CATCHER LOOK LIKE DOG MEAT

———————

This story from Denver in 1901 doesn't have much to do with Mark Twain—except as evidence of the extent of his fame as humorist. Nevertheless, it would seem a shame to leave it out. Moreover, it makes a nice bookend to the articles about San Francisco's Bummer and Lazarus toward the beginning of this volume.

———————

Denver's ever unpopular dog catcher tackled probably the toughest proposition of his career yesterday when he tried to catch the two Marks, mastiffs.

The two Marks are well known by everyone who resides near Thirtieth and Downing avenues, where their owners Catlett & Hill, keep a saloon. Both are large animals, magnificent

COURTESY LIBRARY OF CONGRESS

specimens of their noble breed, and both have lived too many years not to be "on" to the ways of the wily dog catcher.

One of the dogs is named Bismarck, because of the diplomacy he exhibited when a pup. The other is called Mark Twain, because nothing makes him happier than to provoke people's laughter. He never provoked anyone but what they laughed.

Both dogs had been dozing all day yesterday and were longing for a little excitement. They had begun to pick a fight with each other when Bismarck, whose nose is long, smelled the dog catcher. The man was around the corner. The dog gave a low growl that showed he meant the first syllable of his name. Then he told the other Mark all about it, and Mark Twain leaned close to his ear. It appeared as if he was saying: "We'll make that dog catcher look like a nickel's worth of dog meat."

Just then the cage on wheels rounded the corner and the subject of the apparent discussion crawled down from the box. He held his net behind his back and said, "Good doggie." Bismarck evidently did not thank him for the compliment, for he uttered a canine cuss word.

Pretty soon Bismarck was squirming in the meshes of the dog catcher's net. Mark Twain stood by and gave him the dog laugh.

Bismarck allowed the catcher to pull him near the cage, but just as he was half way in the door his humorous brother took a bite out of his captor's coat-tails.

The dog catcher dropped Bismarck and would have caught Mark Twain only Mark wasn't there. He had joined his brother, and both were trolling joyfully down the street towards the smelter.

Mr. Catlett said that he owned a ranch near Brighton, and that the dogs would go there on a vacation until the dog catching days were over.

ACKNOWLEDGMENTS

Like many books, this one was long in gestation before it came together. As a lifelong lover of animals, I'm almost always on the lookout for an excuse to write or edit an animal book, but I can't say exactly when the idea for this volume first occurred to me. To be frank, my first idea for a Mark Twain animal book was to be a collection of his writings about cats. I even managed to persuade Lilian Jackson Braun to agree to contribute a foreword to such a book after she had used one of my own books as a prop in her *Cat Who* mysteries. Unfortunately, I allowed that idea to languish so long, Lilian moved on to another dimension before I did anything about it. Meanwhile, my good friend Mark Dawidziak and I had begun kicking the cat-book idea back and forth. When he was finally ready to act on a cat book himself, I gave him my blessing—with one condition: If his publisher ever expressed interest in a similar book on Mark Twain and dogs, I was to get first dibs on it. Later, when Mark's wonderful agent, Charlotte Gusay, started beating the bush in search of a publisher for the cat book, I thought, why wait? I guess I was feeling a little left out. Long story short: At Mark's suggestion Charlotte took me on as a client and began flogging our cat and dog book proposals together. She soon snagged two pairs of offers. Meanwhile, I tried juicing things up a little more by preparing a third proposal, for *Mark Twain for Horse Lovers*. That proposal is an equine gem, by the way, but it's on hold for the moment. For now I'll merely say that if you like horses as much as you like dogs and cats, another treat may be in the offing.

However, I'm getting off the subject of acknowledgments here, so I had better begin by thanking Mark and Charlotte for their help and encouragement. I also owe prodigious thanks to Holly Rubino, Lyons Press's senior editor who has guided Mark's and my books through publication. As one who has published many books, I can attest to how important it is to work with a skilled editor who doesn't have to fake her enthusiasm for a book. I should also thank Julie Castiglia, my former agent for the many years she helped push my writing career along. Good luck in your retirement, Julie!

I must also thank Mallory Howard and the staff of the Mark Twain House and Museum in Hartford, Connecticut; Melissa Martin and the editors of the Mark Twain Papers and Project at the University of California's Bancroft Library in Berkeley; and Greta Lindquist of the University of California Press for their help in securing pictures and texts and granting me permission to use them in this book. Another major source of illustrative material was the Prints & Photographs Division of the Library of Congress. This book has also been greatly enhanced by newspaper articles I was able to find through the invaluable propriety website genealogybank.com. Among friends and colleagues who lent their help, I would like to thank

Tim Champlin, Michael Golub, Janice Loshin, Kevin Mac Donnell, and Barbara Schmidt.

Finally, I'd like to express my gratitude to Mark Twain's youngest daughter, Jean Clemens, for ensuring that dogs would always be a vital part of her father's domestic life. As her family's most ardent dog lover, she certainly deserves some recognition. When I decided to dedicate this book to her memory, I thought she had been the only member of Mark Twain's family not to have a book dedicated to her by her father, and that I would thus have the privilege of being the first person ever to dedicate a book to her. However, I eventually recalled something I had known before: Mark Twain had meant to dedicate *Tom Sawyer Abroad* to Jean in 1894, but due to a mix-up, his dedication didn't make it into the book, which his own company published. He then intended to put his dedication in the book's second edition, but his publishing company went bust before a new edition came out. The book later went through many editions with other publishers, but his dedication was forgotten until nearly nine decades later, when it was found among his papers and put in a new University of California Press edition of *Tom Sawyer Abroad*. That book has lots of lions and camels and fleas but no dogs. I like to think Jean would have preferred my book.

TEXT CREDITS

1. Hunting Dogs
From "Chapters from My Autobiography," *North American Review*, 1 Mar. 1907.

2. A Vastly Funny Anecdote about a Dog
From *Life on the Mississippi* (Boston: James R. Osgood, 1883), chapter 13.

3. No Puppyish Levity
From "Another Lazarus," San Francisco *Daily Morning Call*, 31 July 1864.

4. Exit Bummer
From "Exit Bummer," *Californian*, 11 Nov. 1865; reprinted from *Territorial Enterprise*, 8 Nov. 1865.

5. General Miles and the Dog
From "Chapters from My Autobiography," *North American Review*, Dec. 1907.

6. The Terrier and the Oyster Crackers
From "Twain Retires," Burlington *Hawkeye*, 7 Feb. 1878; from *New York Sun*, 26 Jan. 1878.

7. No Dog Left Behind
From *Life on the Mississippi*, chapter 30.

8. Bicycles vs. Dogs

From Mark Twain's "Taming the Bicycle," in *What Is Man? And Other Essays* (New York: Harper, 1917).

9. Lively Times for the Family Cats

From a letter to Jane Lampton Clemens, 24 July 1887, Courtesy of the Mark Twain Project, The Bancroft Library, University of California, Berkeley.

10. Entertaining Watch Dogs

From Paine's *Mark Twain: A Biography*, chapter 274.

11. Mark Twain and the Trick Dog

From "Mark Twain and the Poodle," *Dallas Morning News*, July 25, 1909.

12. The Last Family Dog

From "The Death of Jean," *Harper's Monthly Magazine*, Jan. 1911.

13. A Dog with Genius in Him

Mark Twain published the jumping frog story under several different titles, each with minor differences. This passage is taken from *The Jumping Frog* (New York: Harper, 1903), which Fred Strothman illustrated.

14. A Living, Breathing Allegory of Want

From *Roughing It* (Hartford, Conn.: American Publishing Co., 1872), chapter 5.

15. A Dog of a Grave and Serious Turn of Mind

From *Roughing It*, chapter 38.

16. The Dog That Warn't App'nted

From *Roughing It*, chapter 53.

17. An Awful, Solid Dog

From *Roughing It*, chapter 55.

18. The Bull Pup with a Glass Eye

From "Mark Twain Gone Abroad," *St. Louis Republic*, 1 Apr. 1894.

19. The Most Precious Dog in the World

From *Following the Equator* (Hartford, Conn.: American Publishing Co., 1897), chapters 8 and 19.

New Zealand anecdote from *Mark Twain's Notebook* (New York: Harper, 1935), 261.

20. A Reptilian Kind of Dog

From *A Horse's Tale* (New York: Harper, 1907), chapter 6.

21. Rules to Save the Canines

From "Mark Twain on the Dog Question," San Francisco *Daily Morning Call*, 9 Dec. 1866.

22. The Story of the Good Little Boy Who Did Not Prosper

From "The Story of the Good Little Boy," *Sketches New & Old* (Hartford, Conn.: American Publishing Co., 1875).

23. A Dog Meretricious in His Movements

From *Roughing It*, chapter 27.

24. Outfoxing the Fox Hunters

From *Following the Equator*, chapter 20.

25. Camelot—an Uncongenial Spot for Dogs?

From *A Connecticut Yankee in King Arthur's Court* (New York: Charles L. Webster, 1889), chapters 2 and 5.

26. How "Pudd'nhead" Wilson Got His Name

From *Pudd'nhead Wilson* (New York: Charles L. Webster, 1894), chapter 1.

27. A Judgment

From Mark Twain's "'The Enchanted Sea-Wilderness," *Mark Twain's "Which Was the Dream?" and Other Symbolic Writings of the Later Years*, edited by John S. Tuckey (Berkeley: University of California Press, 1966), 76–80. Reprinted with permission of the University of California Press.

28. A Dog's Tale

From *A Dog's Tale* (New York: Harper, 1904).

29. The Poodle vs. the Pinch Beetle

From Mark Twain, *The Adventures of Tom Sawyer* (Hartford, Conn.: American Publishing Co., 1876), chapter 5.

30. "Amen" to the Howling Dog

From *Autobiography of Mark Twain*, vol. 1 (Berkeley: University of California Press, 2010, 416–417). Reprinted with permission of the University of California Press.

31. Why Dogs Aren't Welcome at Funerals

From *Huckleberry Finn* (New York: Charles L. Webster, 1885), chapter 27.

Note about Hartford newspaper from *Autobiography of Mark Twain*, vol. 1, page 622.

32. Hounds Like Spokes of a Wheel

From *Adventures of Huckleberry Finn*, chapter 32. ("Slave" has been substituted in two places for a now-offensive word for African Americans.)

33. Even Dogs Love a Parade

From Mark Twain's *Pudd'nhead Wilson & Those Extraordinary Twins* (New York: Charles L. Webster, 1894), chapter 3.

34. A Passionate Fondness for Dogs

From "The Sandwich Islands" (lecture first delivered in 1866), in *Mark Twain's Speeches* (New York: Gabriel Wells, 1923), 10–11.

35. The Celebrated Slumping Dogs of Constantinople

Main text from *Innocents Abroad* (Hartford, Conn.: American Publishing Co., 1869), chapter 34.

Quote in editor's note from "'The Dogs of Pera," Washington, DC, *Evening Star*, 8 Feb. 1913.

36. German Corps Dogs

From Mark Twain's *A Tramp Abroad* (Hartford, Conn.: American Publishing Co., 1880), chapter 4.

37. A Bark That Stabs Like a Knife

From "Mark Twain at Aix-les-Bains," *Chicago Daily Tribune*, 8 Nov. 1891.

38. "Having" a Dog in Italian

From Mark Twain's "Italian with Grammar," in *The $30,000 Bequest & Other Stories* (New York: Harper, 1906), 192–193.

39. Love among the Ruins

From a letter to Joe Twichell, 25 Apr. 25, 1892, Courtesy of the Mark Twain Project, The Bancroft Library, University of California, Berkeley.

40. "Dog" in German

From *Tramp Abroad*, appendix D.

41. Loaded for Bear

From a letter to William Dean Howells, May 12–13, 1899, Courtesy of the Mark Twain Project, The Bancroft Library, University of California, Berkeley.

42. An Unsuitable Dog for Elephant Hunting?
From *Following the Equator*, chapter 45.

Quote in editor's note from Mark Twain's "Instructions in Art" in *Europe & Elsewhere* (New York: Harper, 1923), page 323.

VI. LESSONS WE CAN LEARN FROM DOGS
The line about a sleeping dog is from Mark Twain's letter to Margery H. Clinton, 18 Aug. 1908, Courtesy of the Mark Twain Project, The Bancroft Library, University of California, Berkeley.

43. Benevolence and Its Rewards
From Mark Twain's "About Magnanimous Incident Literature," *"Tom Sawyer Abroad," "Tom Sawyer, Detective," and Other Stories, Etc., Etc.* (New York: Harper, 1896).

44. How a St. Bernard Saved the Day
From *Following the Equator*, chapter 45.

45. Mark Twain Teaches an Airedale a Lesson
From "Providence Dog Show Attracts Hundreds," *Pawtucket Times*, 7 Apr. 1917.

46. Mark Twain Makes a Dog Catcher Look Like Dog Meat
From "Two Smart Dogs Elude the Dog Catcher and Scare Him," *Denver Post*, 9 June 1901.

ABOUT THE EDITOR

R. Kent Rasmussen is a retired reference-book editor and now a full-time writer who lives in Thousand Oaks, California. A graduate of the University of California at Berkeley, where the Mark Twain Papers are housed, he also earned a doctorate in history at UCLA, where he later taught and worked as associate editor of the Marcus Garvey Papers. In addition to editing scores of reference books on a wide variety of subjects, he has written extensively on history and on Mark Twain. *Mark Twain for Dog Lovers* is his eleventh book on Twain, and he is currently working on three more with still others waiting in the wings. The recipient of numerous awards for his reference books, he was honored with recognition as a Legacy Scholar in the *Mark Twain Journal* in 2015.

Rasmussen is well known for his books on African history but is even better known as the author of the award-winning *Mark Twain A to Z* (1995, revised as the two-volume *Critical Companion to Mark Twain* in 2007). Readers of Lilian Jackson Braun's *Cat Who* novels should recognize *Mark Twain A to Z*, as it is the book Jim Qwilleran is given for his birthday by his girlfriend Polly in *The Cat Who Sang for the Birds*. It is also the book on which Qwilleran's Siamese cat Koko likes to sleep in that novel

TIM CHAMPLIN

and its sequel, but this is not to suggest there is anything soporific about the book. Indeed, it and Rasmussen's other books have been praised for their compelling and often lively writing, which are on display in the present volume.

Rasmussen's other books on Mark Twain include *Mark Twain's Book for Bad Boys and Girls* (1995), *The Quotable Mark Twain* (1997), *Mark Twain for Kids* (2004), *Bloom's How to Write About Mark Twain* (2008), *Critical Insights: Mark Twain* (2011), *Dear Mark Twain: Letters from His Readers* (2013), and *Mark Twain and Youth* (2016), which he coedited with Kevin Mac Donnell for Bloomsbury Publishing. Among his other recent books is *World War I for Kids*, in which he indulged his lifelong love of animals with an entire chapter on the dogs, horses, and other critters involved in the war. Readers of that book may be surprised by the large number of dogs involved in the war and the important roles they played in combat. Rasmussen's many other publications include introductions and notes in the Penguin Classics editions of *Tom Sawyer* (2014), *Huckleberry Finn* (2014), and Mark Twain's *Autobiographical Writings* (2012). His current projects include a book on Mark Twain and movies he is writing with Mark Dawidziak, the editor of Lyons Press's *Mark Twain for Cat Lovers*.